Inner Motivation

A Step by Step Guide to Achieving Your Goals

(Spiritual Advice on Achieving Success in Life, Regardless of Your Concerns)

David Stinson

Published By **John Kembrey**

David Stinson

All Rights Reserved

Inner Motivation: A Step by Step Guide to Achieving Your Goals (Spiritual Advice on Achieving Success in Life, Regardless of Your Concerns)

ISBN 978-0-9948647-3-4

No part of this guidebook shall be reproduced in any form without permission in writing from the publisher except in the case of brief quotations embodied in critical articles or reviews.

Legal & Disclaimer

The information contained in this book is not designed to replace or take the place of any form of medicine or professional medical advice. The information in this book has been provided for educational & entertainment purposes only.

The information contained in this book has been compiled from sources deemed reliable, and it is accurate to the best of the Author's knowledge; however, the Author cannot guarantee its accuracy and validity and cannot be held liable for any errors or omissions. Changes are periodically made to this book. You must consult your doctor or get professional medical advice before using any of the suggested remedies, techniques, or information in this book.

Upon using the information contained in this book, you agree to hold harmless the Author from and against any damages, costs, and expenses, including any legal fees potentially resulting from the application of any of the information provided by this guide. This disclaimer applies to any damages or injury caused by the use and application, whether directly or indirectly, of any advice or information presented, whether for breach of contract, tort, negligence, personal injury, criminal intent, or under any other cause of action.

You agree to accept all risks of using the information presented inside this book. You need to consult a professional medical practitioner in order to ensure you are both able and healthy enough to participate in this program.

Table Of Contents

Chapter 1: Ignition Point 1

Chapter 2: Dealing Challenges 50

Chapter 3: No Void! 74

Chapter 4: Planting The Seed 88

Chapter 5: Metamophosis 103

Chapter 6: The Significant Difference... 117

Chapter 7: How Shadow Work Works.. 123

Chapter 8: Finding Yourself 129

Chapter 9: Navigating Your Triggers..... 163

Chapter 10: Pain And The Inner Child .. 174

Chapter 1: Ignition Point

"The secret to living the life of your dreams is to start living the life of your dreams today, in every little way you possibly can." -- Mike Dooley

SOMETHING SOMEWHERE

"In the dim background of our mind, we know what we ought to be doing but somehow we cannot start." William James William James

I'm sure you've got some idea at the moment. A lot of thoughts are going through your mind. I used to be like that until I made a brave decision to take a step towards working on something. There are too many thoughts within the mind of a person could lead to mental breakdown. One of the best ways to ease you mind would be to establish the first step by focusing on your current situation and what you're. Many people spend their productive life time making plans, preparing and then never taking action. At the exhaustion stage, their strength and energy are lost and they would rather they'd done it earlier than this point. In the worst case, a lot of end up planning to die and hoping the breeze of the sea is peaceful. It's never a better time to throw the net. Fish don't fly, so it is imperative to lunch your fishing net. If you wish to be a horse and all begging people own at minimum one.

The goal is to get to the point where you can ignite your dreams. This book will inspire you to inspire yourself to turn on the ignition to your reality. There's something to complete!

"Allow you to start as a beginner. Nobody starts out being exceptional." -- Wendy Flynn

This is a real-world example, so you will be able to adjust to the frequencies of this work piece. It will be a base basis for any ideas or the inspiration pack within this book. The car is equipped with an engine. The engine is actually performing its function to make the vehicle move using energy conversion processes. Energy conversion, also known as transformation inside the engine is a transformation process that converts one type of energy into the other. It is a process that produces a changes within the engine's system. the engine.

In the internal combustion engine of the vehicle converts chemical energy contained in gasoline as well as oxygen to the thermal (heat) power. This energy is converted into a linear motion which activates the mechanical energy systems that cause a rotational movement of various mechanical components. The energy is then converted into mechanical (kinetic) energy is then transferred to the different engines or propellers in order to make the wheels turn. In the end, frictional interactions between the tyres and the road can enhance the motion of the vehicle. This isn't a way to impart knowledge about mechanics. It's all about what this situation means to the daily life of humans. All existing systems derive their actions indirectly from human nature. They operate according to structure of energy transformation as well as the improvements made created by their inventors.4

Internal combustion is not able to occur by itself. You will now understand how important the ignition source of your vehicle. It draws power from the battery by the process of conversion to light the ignition plug. It is not possible to ignite until the plug is able to generate an ignition. In the event that the ignition fails, owners can choose to start the engine in the event that the system allows.

Do you not want to press the button immediately and embark on your new journey? The power of procrastination does not allow you to ignite the spark. It isn't the catalyst to ignite the flame. In order to set the idea into the right direction, start with turning the key, and let the process of combustion begin. The energy you possess is within the very thing you are. There are people who just want to light the fire but and not participate in the process of combustion. Take note that even thinking of ideas, a plan or plans doesn't guarantee that you will succeed until you are in the field, and you pull the plough.

"The secret to living the life of your dreams is to start living the life of your dreams today, in every little way you possibly can." -- Mike Dooley

SELF-DRIVE - REAL ORIGIN

"The beginning is the most important part of the work." Plato. Plato

The nature that we all possess as humans is derived from the nature (the creator). The biblical account of the creation that was narrated by Moses provides the source of motivational self-motivation. According to Moses, "In the beginning God created the heavens and the earth." Prior to the creation of the world, God was in existence. A significant factor must have been the reason for the creation of Heavens as well as the Earth. A vision was in the air, begging to be realized. It was so large it required the designer come up with a way of getting it. The man was the vision. In this way, you'll be able to see that everything human being is a in the realm of vision. He represents the energy. Much like the creator and the Universe, man is filled with dreams that beckon for execution. The moment we go out today is due to a vision being implemented. Every work of science, art and technology result from vision. What are you able to observe?

If a vision has been given an appropriate amount of amount of energy (provision) is put into it to enable it to work. The process of achieving an objective begins with an impulse that is boosted through the force of self-motivation. Internal combustion is required.

The Creator drives himself. HE initiated in the process of creating the plan by pressing the ignition button, which created the Heavens and the Earth. There is nothing that can exist until it is accomplished. work is required. The true origins of self-drive starts from the beginning. You have a lot of energy inside the person you are. This energy is needed to help you make your idea work. It is essential to draw value from this energy, and then get to the work in creating something. Make value!

"Do what you can, with what you have where you are." -- Theodore Roosevelt

ACTION IN THE BEGINNING

"I won't stop working until my name becomes a verb." DJ Kyos

The goal of this study is to guide you through the fundamental principal of self-motivation. The very first step ever taken took place by God. An example of action from the Genesis story shows the importance of self-motivation's ability to motivate.

"..."The Spirit of God was reflected on the surface of the seas." (Gen. 1 2)

Do you have any questions about the reason God could not exert influence over the natural world? There is no doubt that a successful doesn't end until it's flavored by a specific element. The thing that caused God to get involved at the start was an inner drive. It is a concept I define as self-motivation. The reason for this is the energy that is driving the system. And this is the self-motivation power.

In the next chapter, we'll be looking at "Challenge ". The whole thing could have gone as planned. The lesson is huge that will stir your soul. The action is triggered by the nature-inspired reaction. If there's an occurrence of reaction, you must take action. I've had a good amount of actions in the face of a challenge caused by the natural world.

What do you think? "The Earth was without form and was void. there was darkness on the surface of the sea. ..."

only option was action "...and the Spirit of God took over the face of Waters. Then God told God, let there be light."

It is the most inspiring part of the idea to create a human. The need for action is a must. It's in the course of doing that new concepts are created. Are you sure that you've got an idea? You believe you've got the priority order for trying them out? It's not true! The problem is that when you decide to take action that you find that you need modify your strategy in order to get out. Moses has shown in this enthralling piece of history that the process of creation was made through action.

If God began to act in order to start the process of implementing His plan What are you doing? HE has given each creature the ability to act. It is the action that speaks more loudly than thoughts!

"You will never win if you never begin." Helen Rowland. Helen Rowland

TURNING THE IGNITION KEY

"A time comes when you need to stop waiting for the man you want to be." Bruce Springsteen Bruce Springsteen

One of the key lessons I gleaned from the initial idea of creation was the fact that every man is able and has the ability to design the world in which he lives. "In the beginning God created the Heaven and the Earth." The wind that surrounds is never going to stop. so you'll be able to create worth from it. The only thing you have to do is build the windmill.

What's your mission declaration? There are many individuals suffer from delay. It seems like I understand your perspective. This isn't going change anything. "When your aims are too high and almost becoming impossible to reach, dear create a stepping stone!"

"The way to get ahead is to get started. One of the keys to starting is breaking down the complex projects into smaller, manageable ones before tackling the initial task." -- Mark Twain

It is first your obligation to build the earth and heavens of your company, plan and plans. Moses mentions of the first step of the work that God of the universe. The force greater than yourself, and that exists within you needs to tap your back and push you into action regarding your goals. One of the biggest obstacles to man's achievement is the power of "beginning. These forces are accompanied with a myriad of issues. The most common questions are who do I talk about this concept with? Who is going to listen? What should I do to begin - I'm new to the field. Where do I begin? Are there any criticisms? What if I never get to the highest point? If I fail, what do I do? If you don't get the answers you want eventually, you end up inside the bag or continue working on. Not so!

Your success in life will be largely determined by the responses you provide to the questions that you put to yourself. Only a driven self to offer positive answers to the negative questions. For starters take note of the fact that you are the person asking the question and not you are the person who is answering. What answers will you provide to questions that are within your own mind? These are your worst sacrificial acts. They are the foundation for your faith or the foundation for despair. The world is full of hope!

It is not possible to find anyone who could be as discouraged as you. When I am preparing to accomplish any thing, I put my trust on myself, me as well as God. Man's limits depend on the size of his responses to capabilities and his personal characteristics. Your actions are the most powerful catalyst for redefining your personal existence. All your plans will be useless they aren't implemented. This is the right best time to crank the key!

If you're not able to begin big then start small. It doesn't mean that you're not a small person. Your only goal is to take an initial step toward achieving the lofty goals you have set. Visions are as large as the eyes can perceive but not the way people imagine. Future belongs to people who are convinced of the beauty of their visions. Tomorrow isn't here yet. The future is just a second and away from this moment. It is ticking with the clock and keeps floating. The sole reason why you're currently in the same situation is because you've refused to engage the ignition. Take a look at the entire list of amazing men that have walked the earth of earth, and then tell me about any of them who did not start. There isn't a single one!

"Whatever you think or plan you are capable of achieving, start the process. The power of boldness is in its genius as well as magic." -- Johann Wolfgang von Goethe

WHO DO I DISCUSS THIS IDEA WITH?

When there's a dream, thoughts should have a tendency to swell out in order to push out the vision. There is no way to see a vision within the person you are. Take a look at the story recorded by Moses who had a vision to make man. The entire creation process starting with the creation of heaven and earth to the the light of creation, and then to the sequence was a break down of concepts to achieve the vision. If you're planning to establish a company it isn't enough to leap into the market. It is necessary to first establish values that will be accepted by consumers can accept. You will continue practicing your ideas.

How do I exchange my thoughts who can I share my thoughts with? There are a lot of blocks of thoughts circulating around the streets this moment. There is a desire to take a class. You've got some excellent ideas for business. You must definitely talk to somebody about some thing. It is important to learn influence ideas through your own power of choice. The quality of the people who you share your thoughts to is a significant factor in the way it is influenced. Negative people will never be a great selection. Sometimes all that's required to begin the path is provide a little encouraging words. What kind of people whom you talk to about your plans could either help you get closer to achieving your goal or put off the realization.

The first person to be reassured is the person in the person you are. If you plan just wait around for the world to agree with your ideas then you will not get to any place. Because you're not likely receive all the praise and support it is important to realize that you're the creator of your own destiny. You will certainly be forced to look at the positive and negative aspects of this and it's normal.

At this point, you must sit down to make a list of the idea. It has been my experience that I was forced to shift my plan repeatedly in the process of working towards my goals. That's where the action comes into. Some people claim that it's impossible. They don't realize that you're an enormous mass of energies. If they think it's impossible and they'll clearly provide a variety of reasons to support their position. It takes strength of self-motivation in order to make your opinions more influential. If every suggestion given to you is positive, it's not likely to succeed. You will soon realize that the ideas you have aren't working.

You're probably likely to not go to an unknown person and tell them "Hey I have a lot of thoughts. What and when do you want to participate in this?" the first point of contact will be with the people you have in your circle. There are many people who have been dissatisfied by their most trustworthy family members. They are your friends. You are familiar with their approach to minor issues. Therefore, their reaction whether positive or not should come as surprising. You should then inform your relatives, friends and extended acquaintances and others.

A negative reaction is not going to have any negative impact on you, unless you agree to the negative response. It is likely that you will meet the fire lighters as well as the firefighters, that's the way it goes. If they give you strategies which don't work think about how you can take the next one. There are a myriad of ways that the idea of creating the man could have gone wrong. However, there was only one method that made this vision achievable - ACTION.

Your life will be a challenge with humans and natural forces, making it almost impossible to realize your goals. The only thing you can do is assistance - to take actions.

WHO WILL HEAR ME OUT?

Don't be the first one to hear your voice. You must have ears to constantly listen to you. What do you think your thoughts seem to you? Are you able convince yourself that it can be done? The quality of your hearing cannot be measured by the amount of hearing within your head. Only the ears with the correct ear can provide the correct responses. Certain eyes take longer time to interpret the world in a way that is in proportion to the vision you have. Certain minds take longer time to grasp. "There are moments of action when you don't have to let the sleeping dogs lie."

There is a good chance that not all people is going to be a good fit currently. It might take some time for certain people to grasp. Your vision is yours. It is not possible for anyone else to view it or comprehend it as well as you can. Some people are quick to grasp the issues. They could even aid people see things clearly. Based on their personal experiences They share fascinating and inspiring ideas that touch the heart. You might want to rejoice. These people will take you seriously. They could end up being your guides in the end of the day.

"There are also moment of action when you must let the sleeping dogs lie." Based on my knowledge of Moses Creation history, God took a time for himself to work prior to involving other people. You can see this in the words of God "Let us create man." ..." There are times where you have to deal with various issues within yourself. You will find that a majority of them hear your voice and then nod their heads and nod their heads. That's the help you'll get from them. I'm a better at gauging what I do to people who listen to me. I choose to filter my thoughts through a lens of honesty. Certain of the people that promise help might get you into a mess which will force you out of the picture.

Anyone can listen to you, however, not everybody will be able to support the way you would like. My experience has taught me that nobody will support you achieve your goals. There will be those who are against this because they don't want your to do better than others. Others will inadvertently discourage them in the name of motivation. They will tell you it's impossible. A second set will then flow in the same rhythm, and you will take part in the dancing. Be careful. Heartbreak might be coming to your front door. You'll soon realize you're not in tune. In the pursuit of the goals you have set, there are people who were created to support you for one day. Others are created to help the person for during a week. Certain will work for a month, while others are for one year while others for the rest of your life. Certain people just come to light your fire, but they will not be part of the burning process. This is an inherent phenomenon.

If you know this rule, it is less likely that you will feel disappointed. Don't let them go once you are satisfied in their job. The world is a movie. The characters appear on the screen in accordance with their roles. It's impossible to show everyone at all times.

Do not force anyone to participate within your view. It is your responsibility to focus on the vision, not individuals. If you are pursuing people, you'll be living your dream. People who remain are revealed over the passage of time. What I've collected in the quest for vision has been my greatest source of motivation. If you are going to be successful, you need to be in sync with the principles of practical living. There was provision for vision. Creator is the primary visionary. He is the creator of vision. In He is all the provision made.

Being aware of yourself, and being aware of the voice of your creator. These two basic principles constitute the key to living a life of happiness and happiness.

HOW DO I START - I DON'T HAVE EXPERIENCE?

The process can't begin until you have started. The process won't begin before you have started. Start by making your own heaven and earth. These will become the basis of experience. The creation of your earth and heaven is the very first thing that you'll ever accomplish. The accounts of the creation made of Moses is a good example of this. The process encompasses all essential actions you need to undertake. Visions are something that is only achievable through the process. It is essential to have a plan of actions during the process. The way you begin your life will be determined by the degree to which you can detect opportunities. It is likely to be it challenging if you don't notice or even recognize opportunities. It is crucial to recognize when to ignite your spark and put the ignition system to work. There is energy in the plug already. Just a spark from the bulb is the start of the energy transformation process. When I realized my capacity to positively influence others and to write, I began searching for and developing the platform. It took me several years to study the work of great writers. The question should be changed from where should I begin, to how do I spot beginning opportunities (I'm not requesting anyone to write a book. If you've ever dreamed to become an author, you'll always become one.). Every dream has a goal. A man's vision that wants to establish an enterprise in fast food differs from the one of someone who would like to become a journalist. Someone else would like to own an cinema, while another wants is aspiring to be a doctor and another wants to own a fashionable house, and so on. There are many different visions. They'll certainly need a an approach that is different to achieve these goals. Each of us must create their own heaven and earth to realize their dream. Fast food entrepreneurs will first need to learn how businesses work along with other visionary. You may need to go through some form of apprenticeship or training in preparation of the heavens and earth to their dream.

Experience is important too. Certain people were well-served before deciding to be the boss of their own. If you're able to do that with absolutely, you're fortunate. "Opportunity is the mother of all great experience." Many people have become great by gaining firsthand experience. Their experiences are a part of the course of their development. The term "experience" is really an opportunity to be part of. For instance, a person who has bank experience was actually able to work in a bank since the majority of those who study accounting can find work in the account or bank department. Certain may work in other places and this is the location the place where they can take their knowledge. It's the same just like every other job. The experience I acquired as an electrical engineer gained by opportunities. Many electrical engineers with no knowledge because they haven't had the chance. One way or alternative, they have gained exposure to something different.

There isn't a lab anywhere in the world to provide experiences in learning. Only one laboratory exists working. It's not a matter of praying for experiences. The prayer is for opportunities. It's not about experience that will help you begin but it can help with opportunities. In my experience, I've accomplished a lot of items. I have gained everything through the process. If you want to learn, it is essential to be prepared to study.

It's time to start. Look for opportunities. If you don't have any then create one. That's where the self-motivation power can be unleashed. Most of the successful people were not just aware of and take advantage of opportunities. They also created a lot of.

HOW FAR CAN I GO?

It is possible to go to the extent that your capacity allows. The possibilities are endless and often, you're your own limiter by taking on the fear of being uncertain. It is inevitable that you will have some ups and downs. It's the way it is. There is no way to know how long you are from there.

It is necessary to travel on the way. There is no clue of the solution to this query. If you're interested in knowing the extent to which you are able to go begin today. The beginning isn't what counts, it's the capacity to maintain that drive. It is the sustaining drive that comes from your own determination. You must be determined to move on the path of our lives.

There are many who can't or won't go very far. The extent to which you are able to go will depend on the way you begin and how you steer your journey. In the beginning, it's crucial to build your own heaven and earth. Set aside any issues. Don't procrastinate. It is a way to end your destiny. Most people who do not achieve their objectives didn't believe they could achieve their abilities. Force and friction from nature will be against your efforts. Overcome all obstacles that are necessary now. It is essential to master the problem-solving method. God used a problem-solving method when he first created. Once you get started, difficulties are bound to arise. Create strategies and stay on track.

"One who is skillful in strategy is equipped to conquer." (FCMB).

It's in this process that where you create a plan for your travels. If the main reason you are driven has no limit to possibilities that you'll continue. If you are looking to take your ambitions further, you need to work by the principles and establish an example for yourself or the pursuit you choose. Also, you must adhere to the standards. Without a solid foundation, you won't become a leader for too long. If you don't have a standard, it's impossible to stand out or stand the requirements of the test of time. Create a sustainable value chain.

It is a long way even though you don't know the final destination. If a vision is loaded, it can be an instrument for driving. Think about the distance you could go. Make today the greatest day you'll ever get to do sure that you are doing everything right. You aren't stopping at third base. A lot of failures don't happen in the form of accidents. If you're smart, you'll see the signs. If it's necessary to stop it, take control of its influence.

Because you will soon be begin a new journey in leadership (leadership starts when that you start to appreciate your own worth) being a leader is essential. There are certain strategies that are essential for maintaining a goal. These include: authenticity, honesty, humility and optimism. personality, attitude and perception. The list goes it goes on. All it takes is respect of human worth and dignity.

No one can assist you in developing these skills. You can make by yourself. The power of self-motivation can be used to your advantage. You can certainly go long!

WHAT ABOUT CRITICISM?

Critiques are a natural form of friction. Just like frictional force in actual world, they will only serve to hinder your progress thus accelerating your progress. There will be criticism. It is normal to be criticized. They are brainwashed and look at the other side. It is important to accept that you're not flawless. Create a way that is open for criticism to be heard. The most common failures occur in the event that people forget of their existence in the world. Earth is the home of humanity. In any place where humans live there are criticisms. Mental health is required to withstand the wrath of critics.

To ensure standards and improve the quality of products Certain organizations allow for critique. Critique can help make you aware of the different perspectives of life. The world speaks to us, we act and behave like true individuals. It is essential to think critically. Everything has a positive and negative elements to it. Its impact is largely dependent on what you decide to dwell on.It is a little demoralizing to be subjected to criticism, and it will depend on what you do with the issue. Many great people feel the sting of criticism in everyday activities. Be prepared to be criticized. If people don't get your vision are bound to critique the vision. If you don't get any criticism then the whole world is blind. And it is the blind, who can see the product? A vision that is not visible to the public is just a visual.

You need to know how to deal with critique. Positive criticism is as valid as negative critique. Positive criticism can make you aware of those areas that are likely to lose or fail your business to poor quality or an intentional decrease in the quality of your products or services, or by an increase to the standard of quality the products or services that your rivals are providing to customers.

In contrast Negative criticisms are a deliberate attempts and tactics to deter your efforts and make you be unsuccessful. These kinds of critiques have nothing to do with what the willpower of your own can provide. It's got something to do with self-esteem.

"Coming out of yourself is a sure way to make the skeptic have a rethink about." Ubong Essien Ubong Essien

Do you want to be awestruck by people who believe your concept isn't worthy? The best strategies to beat critics should originate from inside your own self. Thinking that there is any criticism, is the first sign of failure.

Surprise those who believe that it's impossible. Particularly those who believe you're insane. "I am the only person who can deliver a straight-edged punch for people who doubt my faith. It is my responsibility to make sure that they know that it's always achievable!"

WILL I EVER REACH THE TOP?

The question of whether you'll reach the peak is not my responsibility to tell you. It is my responsibility to encourage your spirit to release the energy connection and not give you an unsubstantiated belief or even a shaky sense of inspiration. The way to the top is contingent on what top means to you. Nobody has ever awakened to find himself on the high in the sky. Although he may see it in dreams it is necessary to get up and face the reality of life. That is the way of life. The process of life is never ending. The point you consider to be the highest may be the start of a higher level.

"Nobody gets to the top of a ladder without climbing."

If you're willing to work hard, you'll certainly get to the highest point. Being at the top of the mountain doesn't always require you to be in the top spot of the most successful men around the globe. The point is reached where you are a role persona for other people. "The attitude of your mind is the highest height you can ever reach in life." The issue isn't at the summit. It's getting there from the place you're at here.

The people who make it to the top weren't actually trying to reach the top. They focused on generating worth and making this value systems better. Focus more on improving your current position to make it superior. While climbing a ladder, you concentrate more on the step while you walk up the ladder, gradually gaining the next step that will lead up to the summit. The new height can be your next thought, your next lunch with a creative twist or the next plan of action and the next collaboration plan and the next business transaction and on.

This is the first step you're taking to implement your plans, dreams as well as your vision and thoughts which will take you to the destination you'd like to be. However, you won't be able to get there when you haven't started anything. Self-drive is required, coupled with motivation to begin to move forward, and eventually get there. That's right!

The universe is always willing to lend a helping to help you climb. If you try your best and work hard, you will have the beginning point!

WHAT IF I FAIL?

Failure isn't a brand trend that is new. If you are able to keep your focus away from failing, you will not be successful because it is exactly the opposite of failing. Failure fear may be a sign of two things. It could be to boost your level of commitment and to win mentally, or ignore it altogether.

If I'd had one success throughout my career then I wouldn't have any information to share in this publication. My thoughts are derived straight from a source of actual experience. A number of books have described that Thomas Edison discovered 1000 ways by which the light bulb won't work. In the end, failure is the sole achievement - just very few know about this.

If you're afraid of failing is a sign that you're looking forward to being successful. When I make a mistake I'm always looking to repeat the similar things in a new manner. People don't always examine the reasons why they don't succeed. The reason is not that it's required to not fail. You haven't done it the right way. The system is requesting you to consider a different method of operation. Consider a different approach. If you're confident in your thoughts, you will not quit so easily. It will be a desire to repeat this over and over again. It is not considered a failure even if your process does not succeed. It is a failure when you do not succeed in the process.

The fear of failure is one each human being needs to overcome and should not be afraid of. The failure of a person can be a path to unlocking the potential of your own self. If you think that you'll be ridiculed for failing, then you're already a victim of self-sabotage. Your first task today is to remove out of the way of your mind.

The two strategies you need to effectively work on are the failures and the successes. Many people fall victim of their own beliefs. Faith can accommodate both failure as well as successes. Faith is the shining light even when you don't have a way (when the failure is at your doorstep) and it is also an ability to achieve success.

If you aren't afraid to quit, then you're certainly not likely to be able to succeed. It is a matter of how you approach success from outside. If you don't succeed from the inside then you've failed completely. Find out what is your greatest personal challenge. It could be the very first work you have to complete. You need to change your mindset. Your life is usually shaped by our primary obsession. If you have a taste take a break from it. Your life is governed by the rules which you make. Then, it obeys and abides by the laws you create.

"Don't search for more answers Be the answer. The way you were created is everything you'll ever need. Set a goal to not being a hindrance to your blessings that you have. Breathe deeply and remember to enjoy yourself and then begin." -- Jonathan H. Ellerby.

BREAKING INERTIA

"Don't worry if things may seem daunting at first. This is just a first impression." Olga Korbut. Olga Korbut.

The first step is breaking the force of inertia. Inertia is explained by sir Isaac Newton (English Physicist, mathematician, philosopher and mathematician) the laws of motion. Inertia refers to the force that affects an object that is still in place so that it is unable to move or alter its position. When a moving object moves it is the force of inertia that acts upon the object in a way that it continues to be moving. In order to cause the body move the body, external force is needed. In order for the body to stop, a external force must be applied. Inertia forces also have directly impacted human lives. The tendency is to remain inactive or in the same state. These objects won't change until the condition is changed by external forces.

"An object will remain at rest or in uniform motion in a straight line unless acted upon by an external force." -- (Isaac Newton, First Law of motion).

The creator of the historical account of the creation explained how God disintegrated inertia "...and the Spirit of God was reflected on the surface of the water" (Genesis 1:2b). Each human being is equipped with this power of breaking. If you're not taking action or you have to change to the opposite direction that you're going. The inertia will tell you that you shouldn't try, so it is best not to take any action. If you're on the wrong track Inertia warns you it's impossible to stop and take the right change.

External force is necessary for the change to be made. The external force has to be one that will overcome inertia. The car is unable to overcome inertia until the driver puts an external force to the steering mechanism. This force assists the car to move along its path. External force that breaks the resistance in your life is contained within the you. The external force is going to use the self-motivation power and engage. This power is not derived directly from your surroundings instead, it's derived from the internal combustion system in your body.

In addition to the fact that beginners require to overcome resistance and resistance, but those already in the process will require external force from the inside to continue navigating across the road to achieve their goals. External forces are an additional force. It could come as concepts, strategies, plans and plans, etc. The moment the creator began to break inertia His influence remained constant. His vision by external force, which was linked to spoken phrases. Finally, He set His innate dexterity to work to create His vision (Man).

It's time to move. You're in the right direction, and it's the time to take a step ahead and continue to move. Stop the resistance!

"I believe there's something more significant than simply thinking: doing something! There are a lot of people who dream. It's not enough to take the next step and make concrete steps to realize their dream." -- W. Clement Stone.

CHAPTER KEY REFLECTIONS

1. The most effective way to calm your thoughts is to set the first step by focusing on the things you own and where you're. A few people have spent the majority of their lives preparing for, planning and then never actually executing.

2. Certain people just come to light your fire, but and won't be part of the burning process.

3. After a vision has been given an energy proportional to it (provision) is injected in order to bring it into work.

4. Think you've got the priority order for having them played out? This is not the case! When you decide to take action that you realize that you might need change your plan in order to get out.

5. One of the key insights I learned from the very first principle of creation was that each human being has the power and capability to design the world in which he lives.

6. The wind that surrounds you won't cease to blow, and that you could make money from it. The only thing you have to do is construct the windmill.

7. The success you have in your life will be determined by the answers you provide to the questions you have asked yourself. You only need a positive motivated self to provide positive answers to the negative questions.

8. If you're not able to begin big then start small. This doesn't mean that you're tiny. Your only accomplishment is taking the first step to realize the lofty goals you have set. The vision of yours is as wide as your

eyes can comprehend but not the way people discern.

9. The first person to be convinced is the one within your. If you're going just wait around for the world to support your plan then you will not be able to move forward.

10. There are a few who will claim that it's impossible. They aren't aware that you're a huge mass of energy.

11. The world will test you with human beings and various natural forces, rendering it virtually impossible to reach your goals. Only one thing you owe to yourself is aid - actions.

12. There are times where you don't need to leave your dogs sleeping sleep.

13. The world is a film. The characters appear on the screen in accordance with their roles. It's impossible to show everyone at all times.

14. Do not force anyone to participate within your view. It is your responsibility to focus on vision not individuals.

15. Opportunities are the foundation of all wonderful experiences.

16. You are able to go whatever your capability allows.

17. Because you will soon be embark on a leadership journey (leadership is when you start to appreciate your own worth) having the ability to lead is essential.

18. The criticism of others can help make you aware of your various perspectives on the world. It is a way to speak, act and behave like true individuals.

19. The process of life is never ending. What is referred to as the highest point could be just the start of a new phase.

20. The two strategies you need to effectively work on are Failure and

achievement. Many people fall victim of their own beliefs.

Chapter 2: Dealing Challenges

"When life hands you lemons, you can make wine. Relax and watch while the world marvels at what you accomplished. " - (Anonymous).

DEVELOPING EXPERIENCE

"It is the constant and determined effort that breaks down all obstacles." Clause Bristol. Clause Bristol

The main focus for this chapter comes from the story of the creation written by Moses. The account of creation has helped me to realize that challenge does not respect the persona. People fail because the reason is due to the belief that they should not be experiencing a crises. There will be a question such as why me? If it's not me, who else? Everyone is bound to face their number of issues. They have no connection with character.

The world is filled with experiences. Each experience can be gained by experiments. The process of conducting experiments is not possible without the aid of an apparatus. Life is an experiment board, and the challenge is the instrument. In a real-time experimental procedures, there are some equipments that come with technical and complex aspects. As you master them as you progress, the more skilled you'll become. However, in other situations it could be easier to manage and may require less technical expertise. It is exactly the same when it comes to real-world circumstances. The better you're able to deal with technical and complex challenges, the more experienced you will become.

"All existence is an experiment. The more experiments you conduct more, the more you will learn." -- Ralph Waldo Emerson.

Sometimes, the task gets so daunting that one of the most likely choices is to stop. The motivational power of the self comes into play. The source is within. This is the ability to stick-to-it. It is now that you have the strength to embark. You need the perseverance to keep pace with your goal. Moses has shown us in the biblical account of creation, the vision was maintained by inspiration, opportunities determination, and positive thinking. Now, you are better than everybody else.

The reason why you are more knowledgeable over the guy next to you can be attributed to the obstacles that you've faced.

THE GENESIS HISTORY

God is a creator. Every person does. What makes our story unique distinctive is what we've overcome. It is yours to conquer. You're not past time to give up. "A man without a genesis story haven't yet started because there are genesis challenge that are inevitable, they are like broken bridges that needed to be merged for a path way to your place of vision."

If you are contemplating giving up, think about how long it was to get started. Keep your eyes fixed on the screen. Do not let your eyes wander off to the water. The natural forces may hinder you, however you are owed an incredibly high level of motivation. There is no way achieve everything you want one day. Your business's success depends on how focused you're. "Every big success is the accumulation of little winnings." I've got my own story as well. Failure isn't what matters however, what happens when you come face to face the challenge of the possibility of failure. Each successful person has been a victim of failing.

However, failures and people who succeed can be attributed to their capabilities.

I've seen that the word "challenge" does not respect concepts, status or strategies. The sole command language is the action. It has been my experience that the challenge will come. My wish is the capability and a creative thinking to overcome it.

FINANCIAL FREEDOM

"Focusing your entire life on earning money reveals a lack of ambition. It's a lot of work for you. This will not leave you satisfied." Barack Obama. Barack Obama.

There are many people who want to make cash. Today, the main motivation is not to achieve a goal or achieve a vision. It is certain that you require freedom from financial burdens. People who have faced financial challenges do not often begin their journey to financial liberty.

"Your goal is not as lofty If it's only focused on making cash! Poor people chase money and those who are wealthy attract it. One way to create cash isn't to pursue the money, but rather to draw it. When an individual is to pursue riches, it becomes difficult to find." (Anonymous)

Financial freedom is the act of breaking free from the bonds of financial difficulties by establishing the possibility of a steady money flow. One of the reasons people are who are slacking off is the financial burden. The same problem which men who are successful transform into money freedom. It is impossible to be financially at peace if all you care about is in money. A financial problem must be tackled out of your head.

"The darkest hour in any man's life is when he sits down to plan how to get money without earning it." -- Horace Greeley.

Mental poverty is more serious than any other illness. One strategy to overcome the financial burden is to develop the habit of being positive about the money you earn - do not measure your accomplishments by money. Risk today is nothing short of social bonds. It is not necessary to generate additional power. All you need is in your body. Inside you lies the potential to create wealth. Your system must be in a position to carry out the energy conversion.

Success in financial matters is nothing more than an understanding of finances. "It requires financial intelligence to allow you to enjoy financial freedom. Anything you're currently doing which isn't working, just advise you to try things differently (changing your method of doing things)." -- Anonymous.

I've witnessed young people slithering into schemes to make quick cash but leaving the wealth inside the sand in the dark. Wealth is a flow through the body. Even if you aren't making money right now isn't a sign that you're in a state of poverty. This could indicate you're still waiting to be able to use your wealth-creation capacity or perhaps you missed an opportunity.

An income stream that can't sustain itself will not bring financial independence. Money doesn't bring financial freedom. The first step is to get rid of your thoughts. The second step is to pursue a goal with passion and find freedom in happiness.

"The reason for living is simply to live with purpose. If one is pursuing a goal the money will follow." Rick Warren. Rick Warren.

If you are focused on generating value, and making your existence productive, you will see money come in. A majority of people are deficient in their capability to think critically because they're looking to make cash. The most successful people around the world share one thing they have in common: their an ability to think through problems. They solved issues and their solutions increased their wealth.

"Money is the reward you get for solving someone's problem." Mike Murdock. Mike Murdock.

A quick and easy method cannot guarantee your financial security. You will be forced to follow the rules of prediction. Financial freedom is not enough to increase your independence alone. It can is also a way to elevate other people in the sphere of your responsibility because from the value that you bring to others. Your goal, your goals and dreams require greater mental and emotional capacity as well as financial capability.

"For wisdom is a defense, and money is a defense: but the excellency of knowledge is, that wisdom giveth life to them that have it." -- (Ecclesiastics 7:12).

SOCIETAL FACTOR - How to Fit inn

Society is the most significant arena of challenges. The only thing you need to do in order to cope against such challenges is to face the challenges in yourself. The victims of circumstance and the lucky are all part of society. The society doesn't have the power to transform the character of a person. It only has the challenge of throwing it at the man. Your effort in overcoming that creates an improved society. You're the person who can transform your community. When confronting societal challenges using the maximum of the opportunities life has to offer is an benefit.

"When life hands you lemons, you can make the juice of grapes. And then sit back at the world what you came up with. " - Anonymous.

The materials needed to make a difference can be found easily. The trick is to come up with a creative way to utilize the resources that is available to you. One reason you may not have already started is because you wish that life would give you everything you need and more, including money, talent, the ability to think Absolutely everything. You could imagine yourself smile with an exuberance of laughter and say: "I have wrapped them all up in the opportunity that I throw at him every day."

The American singer, songwriter, multi-instrumentalist, record producer, actress, author businesswoman and philanthropist Dolly Rebecca Parton (popularly recognized as Dolly Parton), recorded a song in April 1971 titled "COAT OF MANY COLOURS" the inspiring lyrics put together narrates how she was able to fit into the society through the effort of her mother.

Check out the lyrics and feel inspired by each phrase5.

Over the years, we've seen

I'm still wondering if it's the same over

Returning to the times of my childhood

I remember a bag of rags given to us.

How my momma used the rags she used to make

There were rags in a variety of hues

Each piece was tiny

Then I wasn't wearing any coat

Then it went lower in the fall.

Momma put the rags in a bind

Sewin Every piece is made in love

My coat was made by her various hues

It was a joy to be so proud of

While she sews her clothes, she shared a tale

She had read the Bible from the book, and had been reading

The coat is made up of various shades

Joseph was wearing and she spoke to him.

Maybe this coat will help the

Happiness and good luck

Then I could not be waiting to put it on.

Mama blessed it by kissing it

My coat in a variety of colors

The one my momma cooked for me.

Only made by rubbings

However, I wore it with pride

We didn't have any cash

I was wealthy as could have been.

In my coat, I have a variety of hues

My momma cooked for me.

And with patches on my bristles

Holes on both of my shoes

In my coat, I have a variety of hues

I was rushing off to the school

To see the other smiling

I'm also making fun of myself

My coat is a mix of shades

My momma cooked for me.

It was so confusing. the concept.

It was because I thought I was wealthy

Then I spoke to them about my love for them.

My momma sewn through every stitch

and I told them the tale

Momma said to me that she told me this while she sews

How my coat is a mix is made up of various shades

More valuable than their clothing

However, they couldn't comprehend it.

and I tried to help them look

The other is just poor.

They can only do this if they want to

We now know that we have zero funds.

And I was as wealthy like I should be.

In my coat, I have a variety of hues

My mom made me a cake

I was made just for me.

The lyrics are touching my heart. It is like I feel coded in the lines, the love and satisfaction. It is true that everyone seeks to fit to the norms of social system. It is essential to think creatively and increase the value of life's experiences to give you. To Dolly Parton, it was scraps of fabric, which when paired transformed into a coat with a multitude of shades. The source of this act was The Joseph Coat of many colours. "For every rags nature place before you, there is a coat of many colours."

Self-drive, confidence and a positive mindset to overcome the winds of loss or the wind.

"When life gives you lemon, make lemonade." -- Elbert Hubbard.

DARING CHANGE

"It's not because things are difficult that we do not dare, it is because we do not dare that they are difficult." Lucius Annaeus Seneca Lucius Annaeus Seneca

No challenge, no change! The truth of a test is that it can change your life. The time of fatigue was when I didn't have a problem to tackle. The world will not be in a romantic bed. People who still expect this kind of offer are going to wait for a long time. Since the earth is circling around the sun, so the competition is getting harder. Beginning a business in 1980s isn't quite identical. Today's challenge is just much more challenging than climate change. The global economic and political challenges are more challenging. There are people who died without ever beginning due to procrastination. take the risk to change your mind and try something new now.

The process of change begins within your character. Your personality, your attitude to perception thoughts, your beliefs and orientation, your lifestyle philosophy, your emotional health, your creative abilities as well as your degree of enthusiasm and your connection with the outside world the psyche and your actions and response. When you have the ability to alter many aspects of yourself and in your it will be evident within your whole natural life. The most effective way to increase your odds is to do more improvements. There is no greater challenge for a man than the challenge. Great men face great challenge. This brings them to the next level of success.

"A man who is faced with 20 obstacles is twice as active than a man with only 10. If you're not facing any problem, get down to your knees and ask God, Lord don't you trust me?" - J. John

Take a look back at the Clause Bristol observation, "It is the constant and determined effort that breaks down all obstacles." Record breaking breakers had no other goal than trying to alter something within their surroundings. The Africa continent appears to be an area of fear for both genders who care about the immediate surroundings, yet they are determined to go globally. Each global impact begins with an area of local influence. "Nobody starts from the top unless he/she is climbing downwards." It is as if as you're aiming for the top, it is a risky shift where you're taking the first step toward the height you've always dreamed of. The story of your life will be more vivid due to the challenges you faced in your journey through the course of your life.

"With courage you will dare to take risk, have strength to be compassionate and the wisdom to be humble courage is the foundation of integrity." -- Keshavon Nair.

Thinking Change during his election campaign the Trump's president Donald Trump, America business man and billionaire, made an extraordinary campaign pledge to build America and return her to the glory of old. That is certainly a great level of ambition. In the context of America as the largest power in the world with a strong economy and a thriving economy, anyone can easily say that America has come to the forefront. Many immigrants from the Africa continents as well as other parts of the globe are taking an the journey toward America. However, here's an individual who is thinking about change and stating that America isn't the place it should be. This should be a signal to anytime in your life, you should know that you're not in the place you should be.

Life is constantly changing and is a continual process. It is essential to be thinking about change continually and act in a constant manner. The reason people are in the position they are is due to the fact that they didn't see the brighter future. Each stone unturned will remain without a turn. A promise to make America excellent again suggests that America is an image of itself. If you aren't thinking about change, it is a gradual loss of splendor. Then you're the shadow of you. And then, others who have other perceptions move forward.

If there's no problem then make one. "He who's not faced anything has never faced any obstacle. The "comfort zone" mentality is self-entanglement. America can be great once more and will continue to grow as it has the leaders who consistently push for changes in and a new way of thinking. What are your goals regarding your country? What changes are you planning about your neighborhood? Are the conditions so good that you don't need to change anything? The answer is no. They're not going to stay this the way they are. The biggest African challenges to leadership in politics is that leaders elected by the people do not have a change plan prior to they take over. They only care about power they hold and are willing to do anything to maintain power, so they continue to pursue their power. They don't want to changing. The power isn't what transforms an individual, a place, or a the nation. Change is driven by ideas, and initiatives. The person, the place, or even a nation can be powerful due to how many changes they have produced.

However, regardless of whether or not you believe in change is inevitable or not, it can happen but could cause you to be battered, and perhaps not much better. It's the way of what is happening in my own country as well as Africa generally.

"If you can't change, you won't grow and if you are not growing, you are not really living." Gayle Shecheg Gayle Shecheg

The point of transformation occurs when a problem stirs in a person's mind and the structure of his thinking. Change is not without opposition all over the world. Even here! The world needs now is not just professionalism, but ideas and actions. Any positive shift in you can result in an influx of positive change to the community. "The ripple effect of our action spread in the direction of our future." Each person has the power to positively influence the society he or she lives in or negatively. Natural and artificial forces of nature will test your beliefs or oppose the actions you take. God has surely thought of changing his mind in the beginning. "The earth was void of form and was void. darkness fell over the surface of the depths. The Spirit of God was reflected upon the surface of the water." (Genesis 1:2 2.)

The challenge makes you highly imaginative, bolstered in your thinking creative in your planning and execution, and adjusted to the changing winds. Think about making a difference. We must be aware of our surroundings. There are opportunities all over the world if we adopt a habit of change.

"Don't be afraid of oppositions; remember, a kite rises against and not with the wind." Hamilton Mabie. Hamilton Mabie.

Chapter 3: No Void!

"You don't have assignment in a place where things are always right." Anonymous - Anonymous

FOOLS STATEMENT

"The struggles of life are as a flood from time to time But never stop! If you have to, cry speed up if you have to and sleep in the night if you have to, but ever give up. "I can't" is the verdict of foolish people" -- Anonymous.

There is no way for a human being to perform when he is in a state of deformation. The cause of deformation is in the absence of data. The advice in this book will act as lubricant to your system of life. It is aimed at igniting the motivation in you, and in reviving your spirit of motivation. This book can bring a fire for someone else's. For another, the book may be the catalyst to can break through the intolertia.

"Every problem introduces a man to himself" declared John Mason. The problem you are facing every day has the power to expose you to a side of yourself that you haven't realized. You are able to recognize your capabilities by tapping into the potential of your own reservoir. If you don't find a specific issue to help you, it's due to your inability to recognize the energy connection that was broken within you.

"No challenges of your life will ever be able to leave you in the same as they found you. It will be either more or less. These are just the cost of growth. The challenges of life are designed to help us become stronger, not more bitter. Adversities are a benefit." John Masion. John Masion.

The spiritual or religious aspects of your life don't create a professional expert in handling problems. You only need knowledge and experience. It has been a problem for people to quit in humanity's beginning. In reality, there's "nothing in human nature such as in idea, opinions, thoughts and plans that is left void until there is a quit."

"The purpose of life event is to teach you how to laugh more or not to cry hard." -- Anonymous.

The fool's statement is: I'm not. That's not true. not going as planned is due to the fact that square pegs aren't able to be inserted into round holes. make sure that what you're doing is correct. It doesn't mean it's impossible or it's impossible to. Everyone has the capacity to explode when he has the correct mindset. There is no way to be perfect, however you can become a master.

Take lessons from God Quitting isn't permissible. "I can't" is a self-defeating language. The most compelling message of my personal leadership philosophy is "WE are able!" The simple wording conveys all the power of the solution of problems. The Earth was empty of form, and the center of resource was obscured by darkness. The Spirit of God was moved. Importantly, you must be as active as you can, take on the fight, and engage in the work involved. There is a chance that you'll need to get to the scene. You can take an afternoon nap! But never never give up. "I'm not able to" is the verdict of fools.

"You will give up if you decide to move forward, you will give up even more if you stay where you are." Writer Bob Gass.

SOLVING THE PROBLEM

Any talent God can provide, He given us (we were created in His likeness). Our bodies are perfect copies of Him. Be amazed by the level of complexity and sophistication that exists in the realm of art, science and technological achievements. You may wonder at times what it would take to create gadgets, or work with complicated programming algorithms. The key is problem solving that is God self-made nature infused into the man. God began problem solving at the moment of the creation.

"Everyone is faced with a problem. Success and satisfaction throughout your life are dependent on your ability to assist people solve their problems. People who are successful are problem solvers." Mike Murdock. Mike Murdock.

Jesus Who was born in the human form was a model for His father's problem-solving character. The main purpose of his life was to resolve issues. and to see the world more clearly. There must be a solution to problems (creating value) in order to have a significant impact. Being a problem solver may not mean that you own SpaceX as Elon Musk or becoming an industrialist as Aliko Dangote. One can solve problems by setting up a shop for retail or a saloon. etc. Look up the value chain that you might be a part of today as you progress from there.

"How good anointed Jesus Christ of Nazareth with the Holy Ghost and power: who went about doing good, and healing all that where oppressed of the devil; (solving problems) for God was with him." (Act 10, verse 38 and emphasis on).

Solving problems is your natural trait. The world is full of people who want to be famous. They will go to great lengths in order to destroy lives to sabotage them or manipulate them in order to obtain the results they desire. But not so! Find a solution and everyone will be impressed with that you.

"A path without obstacle will does not lead to a very important way." - - Anonymous

The stone cutter helps solve problems when building. Fisher man helps solve problems by making protein available for food. Anyone who is recognized by their profession has to solve a problem. The ability you have to tackle problems is what makes you famous. Jesus was not popular until he began solving problems. God has given each of us a level of capability and solutions to global problems.

People who avoid difficulties aren't those who wish. Do not say that it's impossible. It's the verdict of fools. A person who is prepared will find a way to get the job done. Do not be surprised!

"You don't have assignment in a place where things are always right." -- Anonymous

CONVERTING OBSTACLES

"When you face challenges You will learn things you think about yourself were not even known to you. Also, you will discover your true beliefs." John Mason. John Mason.

Breakthrough is a fusion of two words taken from the English word break and "through. The word means "any significant advancement, for example, a significant breakthrough or invention that can overcome an important obstacle."7

If obstacles are not present, there will be any breakthrough (breakthrough). The gap between man's accomplishment and the miracle he has achieved is the amount of challenge in front of him. In the face of obstacles, you can achieve incredible innovation, figuring out what you're made of and most importantly, something that is significant. One of the most important steps to a marvel is to overcome the obstacle. For as long as miracles are around the obstacles will continue to exist. The challenge facing an individual can never be more significant than the challenges he faces. The way you react to situations is crucial.

"Your living is determined not so much by what life brings to you as by the attitude you bring to life: not so much by what happens to you as by the way you makes look to what happens." John Miller. John Miller.

In order to overcome any obstacle, you requires a strong force, and this force should be self-driven in fearlessness. Think of a stone-cutter, He isn't worried about the weight of the stone which he's going to cut. He's only worried about the amount of stones he can extract from the stone. Maintain the same mindset. It's the miracle that's the main aspect. You can't achieve any miracle if you don't overcome an the obstacle. If God offers you an opportunity to be awed, He aids you to overcome the challenges.

All that could be transformed into an innovation (miracle) is an obstacle. They can be doors to greater ingenuity and creativity. Anyone who has nothing to gain should not be expecting the unexpected. Miracles are the result of challenges. One of the main goals is there's no way to get over a particular hurdle that it won't lead to a miraculous outcome. It is possible to find a breakthrough solution. You need the force of motivation to conquer the obstacles.

You must be brave, and you will must be able to take advantage of the obstruction to be able to take off.

"The winds are the most significant obstruction to the flight of an aircraft. However, the aircraft needs to be able to take advantage of wind's effect in order to launch." -- Anonymous.

SANITY - NEW APPROACH

"Insanity is doing the same thing over and over again and expecting different result." -- Albert Einstein.

Take a look; yesterday's fight will not be exactly identical this time. A once-popular solution will not work this time around. Actually, you're not the only one trying to get this. It is essential to be clean!

Remember that the complexity of life is constantly changing. Concepts need to be re-evaluated based on the every day routine. Implementing a new method can help you achieve better end result.

"I didn't believe I have special talents, I have persistence ... After the first failure, second failure, third failure, I kept trying."
-- Carlo Rubbia (Nobel Prize winning Physical Scientist).

The Author Moses report of the Israelites exodus is a glimpse into the super-creative and super-dexterous nature God. God created water at the beginning. The Israelites seem to be among his clients (always complain). He broke the sea of red (miracle). In Mara He simply sweetened the water with bitterness to provide the fish water. For another solution to the exact same issue (thirst) the man utilized a fresh method to demonstrate His vast capabilities to accomplish things (create solutions). The new strategy Moses was just instructed to hit the rock and then the water poured out. Another miracle. However, God did not do it just to him. He decided to present an entirely new way of doing things. (the creator) is aware of many ways to create water.4

The stone cutter continues cutting the stone. Each strike will introduce a different strategy. If you keep going exactly the same way it will result in identical results. That's insanity!

Create a new strategy. Each failure you experience can help you understand what strategy will not work.

Thomas Edison's teachers told him Edison had been "too stupid to learn anything." Edison was dismissed from his two previous jobs due to being "non-productive." As an inventor, Edison made 1,000 unsuccessful attempts to invent the bulb that lights. A reporter asked "How did he feel when he had to not succeed 1,000 times? Edison replied, "I didn't fail 1,000 times. It was invented which had 1000 steps."

"I haven't failed. I've only found a million possibilities (approach) which don't work." Thomas Edison. Thomas Edison.

Rate of success is reduced in the event that failure rate decreases. In order to increase the success rate, move the knob for failing continuously until we listen to the voices of many winners and fewer the losers. Thomas Edison isn't just an inventor. Edison was a model of bravery. If I had succeeded in only one try, I'll never be able to create anything in this novel.

"I have missed over 9000 shots during my professional life. I've been a victim of nearly 300 games. There have been 26 occasions I was believed to be the winning shot, and failed. I've failed time repeatedly throughout my career. This is the reason I am successful." Michael Jordan. Michael Jordan.

Chapter 4: Planting The Seed

"Don't judge each day by the harvest you reap but by the seed you plant." Robert Louis Stevenson. Robert Louis Stevenson.

FLOWERS OR SEEDS?

"Which would you rather have: a banquet of flowers or a packet of seeds?" -- Laurie Beth Jones.

What would you prefer to have? Ask Mr. Jones. A lot of people are passionate about the fruits more so than seeds. Flowers are frequently the preferred choice of lots of people. The only thing you need to do to plant and then wait until harvest time is perseverance. Every day is an opportunity to sow seeds. People want to catch fish, but they don't want to learn how to fish.

The author Jeremiah wrote: "You must "...plant gardens and eat the fruits of them.5" When people do not desire to work when only want to earn money the bills, it is bound to be problems (vices). My father's farm turned into a haven of criminals. The farm was a place where thieves sat and waited for the harvest. They eat their new harvest before eating it with my dad (owner of the farm). This was my experience each year. When you're not able to create, you'll consume. In the world, corruption is growing exponentially. Many people desire quick satisfaction.

"An overnight hit. Gain wealth quickly. Instant gratification! We live in an instant era, we want it now. It's not our intention to plant the seeds for granted, we're looking forward to the blooms." John Masion. John Masion.

Stop the envy and move on the playing field. Develop your wealth, develop your skills. There is no entitlement to something you do not work to obtain. It is a noble thing to work like tilling fields.

Take advantage of this opportunity to plant.

Solomon, the wise and knowledgeable author. Solomon wrote "To all things there's an appropriate season and time for every goal in the universe. ....a the right time to grow (invest to develop talent, invest in it and so on) as well as a time to plough up (reap the benefits, relish etc) what is cultivated ...." (Ecclesiastic 3. Verse 1, the emphasis that is added).

God is able to plant seeds within each man. He doesn't want to make you fruitful if He doesn't have seeds planted inside your body (emphasis taken from Moses the creation story) Some look for the blooms created by other people. The wrong way to channel their energy is in order to cultivate and control the seeds of vice.

"One well cultivated talent deepened and enlarged, is worth hundred shallow faculties." -- William Mathew.

OWNING BOUQUETS OF FLOWERS

"Which would you rather have: a bouquet of flowers or a packet of seeds?" -- Laurie Beth Jones

Every seed that you plant provides an opportunity to the harvest. The desire for lazyness can make you want flowers when you are in the vicinity of seeds. There are the most bouquets of flowers as you like if you choose the seeds.

"You are not entitled to something you didn't explore. The evidence of your desire lies when you are in pursue." Mike Murdock. Mike Murdock.

God has granted you a gift or talent. The very first instruction at the beginning of the creation was "Be fruitful and multiply."

Flowers (representing the final product, the result and the success, etc.) aren't able to produce fruit all which is needed is cultivating that natural aptitude or talent and then put it into use.

There is a good chance that you've put at least some effort the process of starting a business or putting your talents to use. The idea could have fallen by the side of the road, the floor of a hill or Thorns but not yielded anything.

The author Mathew recorded the life of the Rabbi Jesus6 (the best success coach) in the story of the sow that illustrates the determination and perseverance of a farmer who had vision to harvest a crop. There were many challenges he faced in his first venture into the fields. However, he was never discouraged.

"But other fell into a good ground, and brought forth fruit, some an hundredfold, some sixtyfold, some thirtyfold." -- (Mathew 13:8).

It's the power of determination! It pays off with gold coins.

"Most people do not realize that they're close to being successful when they stop. Keep in mind that stopping at third base will and adding no more scores than striking out." John Mason. John Mason.

I've learnt lots of things from my dad. He has a subsistence farm. There was always lots of food to give away. Through the entire year we enjoyed our crops of melon, cassava, Okro, corn, the yam barn, and a tiny amount of hunting expertise like trap setting, we always had fresh meat and food at our tables, thereby reducing the price of purchasing. We are not allowed to grow. We had the chance You know what? We buried all the seeds that we could. We were not aware of the fundamentals of plantation. Yet, I watched my father plant strategically by using the traditional methods he learned from his father.

The main point to take away is. When plantation in the morning, rodents have a feast in the field during the evening. In some cases, the rodents attack occurs as the seeds begin to germinate. We tried every traditional techniques of scaring rodents. They thought it was a the way of heaven, but to us, it didn't seem humorous. However, we're certainly not likely to be smashed by birds and rodents. My father has take over the seeds and start plant another time. Then we are able to smile at the harvest. The constant effort of a farmer is among the key ingredients to a successful harvest.

"One among the most effective strategies for success ever taught is to never let up! - Sir Winston Churchill

It's likely that you haven't had the same experience.

PLANTING THE SEED IN YOU

"Don't judge each day by the harvest you reap but by the seed you plant." Robert Louis Stevenson. Robert Louis Stevenson.

Everyday is a chance to start a seed. Seeds are planted in a variety of ways. This could include helping someone achieve their goals or achieving their goals. In the future, someone will come to you and you will be asked "How many people did you help grow their seed by sowing a seed in them." A few individuals are more dangerous than rodents who attacked his father's property. However, regardless of whether you sow or not, there will be the reaping.

"If you think in terms of a year, plant a seed; if in terms of ten years, plant trees; if in terms of 100 years, teach (invest on) people." In terms of a year, plant a seed; if in terms of ten years (Confucius With emphasis).

In this instance you have more to you, more than any other person. "Don't wait for someone to bring you flowers Plant your own garden and decorate your own soul." (Luther Burbank). Whatever you would like to have in your future You must start planting today!

"To plant a garden is to believe in tomorrow." Audrey Hepburn. Audrey Hepburn.

The field of life is the biggest that has ever existed. Everyone is blessed more over the others. All of us have the same chance to grow anywhere, anytime. The majority of our problems stem because we aren't able to take advantage of the amount of space available and to cultivate our fallow land.

We simply look at the flowering plants that are produced by other people.

"Consistent sowing ensures consistent reaping. Each seed plant schedules an harvest." (GSAF). (GSAF).

PRINCIPLE OF PLANTING

"For flowers to bloom there is a need for the proper soil, as well as the correct seeds. Similar is how to create a good mindset." -- William Bernbach

The wise and knowledgeable author King Solomon wrote "He who is observant does not sow, and one who looks at the clouds will not reap. The next day, sow your seed and in the evening, don't hold your hands: since thou knowst not if will prosper, whether one or the other; or if both will be equally great." -- (Ecclesiastics 11:4).

William Bernbach has given an insight into an important aspect to be considered. As a result of the story of Rabbi Jesus The only seeds that can yield will be those that are in the right soil. A good soil is are in the best place that you are able to grow your abilities. Once God starts to support your dreams, He will first take you to an Island to find others with similar goals as well as dreams. Finding the right spot is the very first step towards creating a dream or igniting the spark of a dream. The only way to endure and thrive is in the proper conditions. I've had a large amount of experience in farming. My dad never cultivated on the clay soil. It's a given that it will not last. This is the way you are. It won't be able to last when they are thrown at those who aren't the right individuals.

The other aspect that is part of William Bernbach inspiration talks about planting the right seeds. Many people in the middle of their lives, and are at work doing something wrong (something which isn't in alignment with goals). This may be the result of their lack in self-discovery). Maize isn't planted for the purpose of harvesting the yam. Now is the time to think about it. Naturally, continuously sowing maize will not guarantee that you will reap the harvest from yams. For success in the world, it is essential faith in God and then prepare yourself to work within the realm of your goal. Every device invented, has an inbuilt purpose by the inventor/manufacturer.

Many times, my dad tried to plant onions. The plant failed because of the wrong soil. The person who is in this book, and they might decide to not give up this soil, or even the seed that is not right for them. Self-drive is required and motivation to break through that barrier. The author Paul wrote in his letter to the Galatians, on the importance of knowing what you are sowing.

"...for what a person sows, he will will reap."

THE HARVEST

"All the blooms of tomorrow will be in the seeds that were planted the present. Therefore, it is essential to nourish the seeds of our time carefully." The author is Ekiri Ashien.

Do not forget where you are starting from. It might be a good idea to flip your head the page backwards, and then be tuned into the frequencies of this book. When seeds are sown there is bound to there will be harvest. The seeds may not be able to survive. The way you manage your garden is crucial.

The biggest challenge has been feeding the seed so that it can grow. There isn't any plant that can grow to harvesting in one day. I don't know if there is such a thing in the globe. Every field being cultivated is going to require an enormous amount of work to keep the fields in good condition.

"All men have dreams, and certain of us let dreamers die. But the other nurtures and shields them from tough days...to the sun and light that always arrive. - Woodow Wilson.

The farm my father owned was bordered by farms owned by farmers. Most farmers are forced to leave their property to get rid of. Ours was the most productive farm because we wouldn't even give weed an opportunity. The process wasn't simple. Our passion to harvest the crop was the main motivation. All you require is seeds. The flowers will soon appear. They will naturally grow to rival your seed's to get sun and nutrients. Don't permit it!

"We may be able to count the numbers of seeds in an apple, but we can never count the numbers of apples in a seed." -- Anonymous.

What's your motivation for a flower arrangement or a bag of seeds? Do not be afraid to pursue your goals. Nothing can be achieved in a flash of pleasure. To reap the benefits, it is best to start by planting your ideas or developing a skill and to be a part of this process. Many people began their professional with security personnel, and as they grew older they saw improvement in their own. They progressed to the management levels, become the CEOs and managers of large collaboration. It's not a fairytale. The cultivation process requires sacrifice. Which seed do you plant now? Are you taking the time to enhance your capabilities, receiving relevant education, upgrading your education, attending relevant classes, or learning in a completely new fields, or have a nagging itch for an individual who's struggling to make improvements to be ready for next year's harvest?

We'll look forward to the next chapter."Don't allow weeds to grow in your goals." John Mason. John Mason.

Chapter 5: Metamophosis

"Great opportunities come to all however, many people are unaware that they've been blessed with these opportunities. The best way for maximizing the opportunities is to keep an eye on the events of each day." Albert Dunning

LOOK FORWARD

"Show me a thoroughly satisfied man and I will show you a failure." Thomas Edison. Thomas Edison

Your problem is that you've turned into a step to get to the top of a mountain. It isn't a good idea to gaze at the future. The fool who is rich is an example here.7 He was able to accumulate a little fortunes through chance. This was an opportunity to germinate a seed for the other. However, he's risen to the summit.

It requires motivation to see the future to a long-awaited achievement. Most people are content by the surroundings they have found them. It's just a matter of taking a step up. A happy man will not be more than his surrounding. There's still opportunities to be had. If you stop for breaks to enjoy your merry, it is easy to lose focus.

It is not necessary to be content, just keep digging up fallow land. Find out what's new. Keep pursuing opportunities. Every successful turn is worth an extra. It's impossible to reach the mature stage in your life if you don't be looking ahead.

"Great opportunities come to all however, many people are unaware they've been offered these opportunities. One of the best ways for maximizing these opportunities is to be aware of the events of each day." Albert Dunning

Your life will transform into a metamorphosis. Take your life to the next level. There is no time for rest. Continuous and ongoing change occurs.

"If you can't change, you won't grow and if you are not growing you are not really living." Gayle Shecheg Gayle Shecheg

PABLO THE PIPLINE MAN

My first attempt in my experience of attending the job interview, I thought it was wasted time. Following the test for aptitude, I thought that the next test was going to be a chance for me to respond to questions about my particular field. After that, Miss Regina arrived and delivered the class, and then the teacher played us a video. So long as you've an idea, the opportunity is bound to be there. That's the Pablo and Bruno's tale written by Barke Hedges. It is a parable about the pipeline8.

Pablo and Bruno were a couple in a quaint Italian village. They were the best of friends, as well as they were big dreamsers. They would talk about their dreams for one day, in some way they'd become one of the richest people living in the town. They were both smart and hardworking. They only needed a chance.

A chance came along. The village's mayor was able to recruit two locals to take water from the nearby river to a water cistern on the town square. The job fell to Pablo and Bruno. Two buckets were each emptied by the two of them and headed for the river. At the end of the day, they've filled the town cistern up to full capacity. Village elders paid them 1 cent for every bucket filled with water.

"This is our dream come true!" exclaimed Bruno. "I can't believe our good fortune." However, Pablo was not so certain. The back of his body was aching and his hands had blisters because of the weight of buckets. He dreaded waking up to go to work the next day. He resolved to come up with an alternative method to bring the water that was flowing out of the river back to the village.

"Bruno, I have a plan," Pablo declared in the morning, as they gathered their buckets and headed towards the river. "Instead of lugging buckets back and forth for pennies a day, let's build a pipeline from the village to the river." Bruno was stunned to the point of death. "a pipeline!

Anyone heard of such a phenomenon?" Bruno shouted "We are doing a fantastic job, Pablo I can transport hundred buckets of water every day for a dollar a bucket which equals one dollar a day! I'm rich! At the end of week, I'll be able to purchase an additional pair of shoes. The time the month is over, I will have I can have a cow, and at the end of six months, I will be able to purchase a new house. The best job in the town. We get weekends off as well as two weeks of paid time off each year. We're set for life! You can get out of this by removing your pipe.

However, Pablo did not let himself be dismayed. He was patiently explaining the pipeline's plan to his closest buddies. Pablo could work during the week with buckets and carry them, then spend the rest of the weekend and daytime developing his pipeline. Pablo knew that it was tough work digging a trench in the hard soil. Since he earned his money per bucket, he was aware that the income would decrease. It was also his belief that it would be a few years before his pipeline paid off. However, Pablo believed in his vision and got to work. Bruno as well as others from the village started to ridicule Pablo and calling the man "Pablo the Pipeline Man."

Bruno earned more than twice as much money Pablo displayed his brand new items. The donkey was outfitted with a brand new saddle. The donkey was put aside in his brand new 2-story cabin. He also bought flashy clothes and a fancy meal in the hotel. People called him"Mr. Bruno, and they were cheering when he purchased rounds in the tavern, and were astonished by his jokes.

"Small actions equal big results"

When Bruno was in his hammock at night and on the weekends Pablo was constantly digging up his pipes. In the beginning, Pablo was not able evidence of his work. His work was difficult, much tougher than Bruno's due to the fact that Pablo was working late into the night as well as weekends. However, Pablo constantly reminded him that dreams for the future depend on the sacrifices of today.

Each day he dredged in, inch by inch. The inches grew into a foot, and then 10 feet, 20 and finally 100 "short-term pain equals long-term gain," He remarked to himself after slipping into the hut following another tiring day's work. "In time my reward will exceed my efforts." He considered. "Keep your eyes on the prize," He thought as he drifted into sleep, accompanied by laughter emanating at the tavern of the village to the left.

Months turned into days. Then, one day Pablo discovered that the pipe was halfway done, which means that he will just had to work only half the distance to fill up his buckets! Pablo took advantage of the period for work in his pipeline. In his break time, Pablo watch his old colleague Bruno haul buckets. Bruno's shoulders were more bent than they had ever been. He was slumped with pain and his stride were slowed down by the everyday grind. Bruno became angry and bitter and resentful of the fact that he was bound to carry buckets every day, every day all the time for the rest of his existence. Bruno began spending less time at the hammock and spend more time at the pub.

If the patrons of the tavern noticed Bruno approaching, they would yell "Here comes Bruno the Bucket Man," and laugh when the locals imitated Bruno's posture, stooped and shuffled step. Bruno did not buy rounds nor talk about jokes anymore and preferred to make his home in a dark, secluded corner in a dark corner surrounded by empty bottles.

The day finally came for Pablo and his pipeline was completed! Villagers gathered around the pipeline while the water ran from the pipe to the cistern in the village! The village now has an uninterrupted supply of fresh water, residents from the country come to the village, and the community prospered. When the pipeline was completed, Pablo didn't have to take buckets to work anymore. The water was flowing regardless of whether or not he worked. The water flowed even while he was eating. It flowed during his sleep. It was flowing on weekends while the kids played.

The further the river flowed to the village, and the greater amount of money was deposited into Pablo's pockets! Pablo The Pipeline Man was popularly known as Pablo the magician. However, Pablo realized that what he achieved wasn't a true miracle. It was simply the initial step of a large idea. The reason is that Pablo was a man with bigger goals. Pablo had a plan to build pipelines across the globe!

RECRUITING HIS FRIEND TO HELP:

The pipeline also drove "Bruno the Bucket Man" out of business. it hurt Pablo to witness his old buddy begging to drink at the local tavern. Then Pablo set up a time to meet with his former friend. "Bruno, I've come here to ask you for help." Bruno bent his shoulders and stooped, his dark eyes widened to an averted smile. "Don't mock me," Bruno hissed. "I haven't come here to gloat," declared Pablo. "I've been here to present an excellent business chance. It took me nearly two years until my first pipeline was completed. It was a learning experience over the course of these two years. I'm familiar with the equipment I should use, as well as how to go about digging. I am aware of where to place the pipe. I made notes while I was building and now have a method that will permit me to build a new pipeline faster, after which I can build another.

I can build an entire pipeline in a year me, however what I'm going to do is teaching you to construct a pipeline and then teach other people and let them instruct others.

"Just think we could make a small percentage of every gallon of water that goes through those pipelines." Bruno realized that he was looking at the huge image. They embraced with shock and awe as if they were old buddies.

Years passed. The world pipelines of their respective countries were putting billions of dollars to their accounts. In the course of their travels in the countryside Pablo and Bruno were passing people from villages across the country carrying buckets. They would stop and recount their tale and then offer to assist them create the pipeline. However, the majority of bucket owners would deny the suggestion. "I don't have the time." "My friend told me he knew a friend who's uncle's best friend tried to build a pipeline and failed." "Only the ones who gets it early make money on a pipeline." "I have carried bucket my whole life, I'll stick to what I know." "I know people who lost money in a pipeline scam."

Both men were content with living in a society with a bucket-carrying attitude, but only a tiny fraction of people could ever grasp their vision. The hard work alone won't get us the kind of success we desire. It is imperative to take advantage of the chance and understand how to create an avenue that will work for us over the longer term.

"Opportunity is missed by so many people because it dressed in overall and looks like work." Thomas Edison. Thomas Edison.

Chapter 6: The Significant Difference

"Action is the foundation key to success, to guarantee it; you act as if it were impossible to fail because it is in doing ordinary things in extra ordinary way." The foundation of success is Anonymous.

ADDING EXTRA

"The difference between ordinary and extraordinary is the little extra." -- Zig Ziglar

A Irish dramatist, writer, and critic once stated: "When I was a young adult, I realized that nine of 10 activities I took part in failed. I did not want to be an unqualified failure, which is why I put in ten times as much work."

When you're in the field, you have to try to be a part of the change. Many people do not know about this approach. However, every famous person has employed the strategy. There is nothing

I've ever done as people do it. There is always a strategy for how I can make it distinctive by way of concepts and strategies. The requirements of applying a new methods in the previous section.

The fact that I was able to distinguish two times while my time at school wasn't as magical as some students thought it was. I followed the triangular structure of daily life. From the house to class and back to the library and then back to my home from the library (at time, stopping on to attend church) and work goes on. It was evident that the extra effort was noted on my school's grades. Once I was able to accept routine life, I began to slide down the slope.

An untrained boss or manager will not be as effective than the person who is doing all the work. It's not enough to start. You need a passion and determination to take on more action. It is essential to push this to the next step. Don't compare yourself with those who have no problem employing the standard strategies. They will soon be left behind by the world. these people in the dust.

One of the costs of being good is the ability to perform things in a way that is always unique. It is only possible with a little extra effort, the extra time, and sleepless nights. Change your performance right now. It is still possible to influence and elevate your business up to a higher level. Make sure you do the extra!

"Action is the foundation key to success, to guarantee it; you act as if it were impossible to fail because it is in doing ordinary things in extra ordinary way." -- Anonymous.

LEARN FROM MR. BEN

There is nothing that changes when you do never change anything. Effective time management can allow you to make the best utilization of your time. When they are exhausted from chasing things that don't matter, the person finally informs you that they've been working. Was it doing what? People who do not value their time cannot make maximum usage of it.

It is a commonplace school normal farmers, common musicians, normal footballers, normal teachers normal politicians, regular leader, and even extraordinary people. What differentiates them is in the autonomous nature. Make sure that you are prioritizing the things that matter. Have fun at you're looking for a relaxing time. You can play the game. Socialize with friends and women. All work and no play has made Jack dull."You aren't Jack. Jack might be smarter today. Be aware of your the important things!

I've learned a lot from Ben Carson (America retired surgeon as well as author and politician) In his book"THE GIFTED Hand" He shared the secrets of academic success that led him to become an international neurosurgeon. Ben Carson, the dull kid Ben was unable to do anything until his mom (Sonya Carson) led him through an remarkable existence. Sonya removed Ben from watching the television unless there were relevant shows to allow him to take on his writing work.

Ben is a success story both in academia and professional fields (successfully dissociating conjoined twins) isn't a miracle. God is awestruck by any effort. God rewards all efforts. Ben attributes his mother Sonya Carson to his accomplishments in his life, when he stated "I did not just see and felt the changes that my mother's influence made on my life, but I have lived through those distinctions as an man."10

The most powerful motivation was Ben's determination to do things extra.

"Success is largely dependent on determination and perseverance. That extra drive needed to keep trying or develop a new strategy is the key to success." Denis Waitley

Chapter 7: How Shadow Work Works

The Basics of Shadow Work

The process of shadow work consists of confronting your shadow for personal development and satisfaction. It is based on a variety of techniques. In order in order to gain the benefit of these strategies must fully take on what's asked from you.

Prepare yourself to reflect on yourself. Research has proven the value of self-reflection. Stefano et al. found that when employees were given enough time to reflect upon their lessons learned they started to do more than the employees who didn't. In addition, it required about 15 minutes to do this improvement. A different study from the UK revealed that when individuals think about what they would like to achieve, they're not just more productive however, they're generally happier. Self-reflection therefore is essential to grow.

Journaling is an essential component of shadowing within this guide And journaling is yet another technique that has proven to change lives of people. The research suggests that people who write at least 15 minutes every day of their week experience less stress and are happier. In addition, they're more healthy and exhibit more positive immune reactions. Journaling helps you to know you better and make connections with parts of you that may ignore.

The journey can be daunting even at times. It's going to be personal, and you'll have to face aspects of yourself you've never been able to confront. Feelings you experience when you're reading this journal are common as they're signs that you're improving your self-image and moving towards the right direction. If you don't feel uncomfortable then you're not aiming deep enough to create genuine change.

Why Shadow Work?

Shadow work is an excellent option for those who feel restricted by their dark side that hinders their ability develop, flourish, or be a part of the bright side. Shadow work allows you to get into touch with your dark part without giving up on that dark side. Once you have accepted the process done in this book, it are able to encourage self-acceptance and confidence in yourself, and self-love.

The advice and suggestions contained in this book can aid you in improving your connection with people. If you're not paying attention to your inner self it is possible that you feel disconnected from people you know and are you are unable to form important connections you want to create.

The methods this book will teach it will be helpful to even after you've finished all the work in it, and continue to practice several of the methods you've begun through these pages. Writing a diary as well as taking the time to reflect on your own are methods you need to use throughout your lifetime for long-term health. It can be beneficial to any person's life if they are willing to put their effort into.

A Note About Professional Help

If you're who are dealing with mental health issues The book's purpose isn't to replace of professional support. The book can help you get in touch with your shadow self. In some instances, you might need for a third party assist you in making gains.

If you feel you may require assistance from a professional, contact us and locate the right professional that is an ideal fit for your needs. When you need help it is still possible to use this guide as an additional source of assistance, and can aid you to make advancements in your own personal growth. It is, however, general enough to require specific assistance for particular problems.

Make sure you take care of your mental wellbeing Without further delay you should begin exploring yourself and discovering the persona you are.

Initiating Thoughts

A few sentences on the reason you've decided to start this project and the goals you'd like to accomplish with your journal.

1. What prompted you to choose this book?

2. What do you envision your life to be as after completing the exercises?

3. Which aspects of your daily life do you struggle the most in?

4. What is the length of time you have planned to devote to this endeavor?

5. What are you likely to be losing if you don't take modifications?

Chapter 8: Finding Yourself

The Basics of You

The most significant aspects of confronting the shadow side of yourself is to learn about yourself beyond mere the basics of who you are.

Answer these questions in order to introduce yourself to the people you shadowing job. It's straightforward to pinpoint certain aspects of yourself like your name, job as well as family and friends However, many more aspects make up your identity that aren't just the ones you have mentioned. To warm yourself up, try focusing on answering some of the most basic questions, and then reflect on the ways in which these fundamental elements are able to reflect deeper aspects of your self. A few of these questions might appear too straightforward however, they can assist you to begin the journaling process, and can be vital to other aspects of your personal identity.

Simple Introduction

1. Your name is what you are, and do you want to be known as?

2. The year you were born and at what age are you?

3. Which country were you born?

4. Which city do you currently reside in?

5. Which color is your most favorite?

6. How were you as an infant?

7. What is your family? Are there siblings? any other significant relatives?

8. You can list the individuals you're closest toincluding family members, spouses, partners and friends.

Interests and Activities

1. What do you do?

2. What are your hobbies?

3. What's your dream date night (or day) going out?

4. What does a perfect meal take on (what do you want to eat what would you eat, who'd be there and where you would be there, etc.)?

5. Which type of media appeals to you (music or TV movies, books etc.)?

Reflections on the Process

1. What are your feelings so in relation to this novel?

2. What are the main worries you are facing as you begin the process?

3. What are you most excited to begin your new journey?

What is Identity?

An individual's identity is what they are. And as your answers to the above questions might suggest the many aspects of who you are. They may seem to be easy to identify. For many, however particularly those who struggle with mental illness, an identity crisis can create a variety of inner conflicts. Being aware of what "identity" means and its significance on your life will change the way you view yourself as well as what you portray about yourself. If you are able to be true to the person you are, your path will be more clear as you are comfortable in your own skin.

There are a lot of misconceptions regarding identity and its meaning that create difficulties for individuals to establish positive relationships with themselves. One of the biggest myths about identity is that it is an object that is easy and inactive. Most people think that having an identity can be as simple as a picture in a photograph identification card. However, it's more far from the truth. Human beings are complex as well as beneath the top layer of our identity we have shadow motives and desires. The shadow of our self determines our identity and the way we perceive our self. There are many layers to us which require lots of concentration to remove those layers.

The person you identify with can change in the course of time, based upon the experiences you have had and your ongoing self-discovery. The nature of your identity is always changing. Even though there are some core aspects of yourself that do not change however, this doesn't mean you can't change. Individuals grow and develop. In addition, they are taught about new concepts, but their lives are shaped by various new situations. If you're in school you may be regarded as a brilliant student. But once you've stopped going to the school, you could still believe that you're smart. However, you might have risen into a smart professional. Humans are constantly evolving and you shouldn't be relying on the identity that has always been yours, so you should keep keeping track of yourself.

As an example, someone could claim to be homosexual because of societal norms as well as defining themselves as straight by the way they behave, but there may be a sense of a deep-seated feeling that exposes the flaws in their image, and the individual might discover that they may be bisexual or gay. They are not changing their sexuality and neither has the way in which they define their self is changing. Therefore, context and the surrounding environment will influence the names they choose to give themselves, and the image they want to appear in the world. That's okay! You can change your perspective of yourself and adjust to learning more regarding what you enjoy and makes you feel happy.

Your surroundings often affect how you perceive yourself. If you're a kid you learn from the adults around you. A lot of the beliefs you hold are those you learned from your the parents you grew up with or from other caregivers who were your first teachers. Naturally, as you get older you'll naturally question the ideas you've been taught however this doesn't mean you shouldn't adhere to any principles you were taught in your childhood. Additionally, those whom you love and admire often determine what you consider to be the right or wrong. If you were a devoted teacher at college, you may change your view of your life and the world based on the lectures they gave you. In addition, it's common for friends to have the same values in life If you're married it's common to find yourself becoming more in line with the values of your spouse. The values of each person are different, however, it's not a secret that people who surround can have an effect on your life.

Your personal identity doesn't just revolve the result of your beliefs and passions. It also includes the things you've experienced. Common, but painful experiences such as loss of a loved one can be very painful in the sense that when these experiences begin to affect your thinking and behave, they may be categorized as trauma. Trama is not only an unsettling experience. it has to have lasting adverse effects on the person. In the case of example, if you lose a loved one and, after an ordinary grieving process and you're able to continue living your life without adverse consequences but you're not in any way affected by the loss. The fact that you don't have trauma does not indicate that you've never experienced a great deal of pain however, it is important to remember that what hurts someone else won't be the same for one. Any physical or emotional hurt that is of any type can have devastating negative effects, but trauma usually speaks to the center of your shadow self.

Trauma alters how you view your self. It's easy to recognize the effects of traumas that are major that include physical abuse or sexual assault. However "small-t" trauma can also be a major influence. They can involve factors like belittling, prejudice bullies, emotional abuse. They do not have the same impact as "Large-T" trauma. The type of trauma you experience encompasses all of the minor injuries that could compound and alter how you conduct yourself It is a kind of trauma that's usually unnoticed and difficult to identify. Since not one major event occurred, you can feel its effects. However, they can hide inside the shadow side of yourself. The person who is traumatized may not even realize they suffer from trauma until you begin working through the exercises through this book and see that your previous experiences continue to influence your life. The book will provide more details about trauma in the coming chapters. However, be aware that it influences how you see yourself.

The shadow you creates can alter the persona you're. It holds on to the wounded areas of your personality and encases these parts into your persona. It is able to take your most negative attributes and transform them into those that are most prominent. We all experience dark sides to us, and it's not good to live in the darkness within, when we allow our shadow selves remain unattended, it's possible to lose sight of our identity and lose track of which things bring us the greatest satisfaction.

Mirror Image

Take a seat before the mirror, and stare at yourself for about five minutes. Once you've finished take a note of what you appear like. At this point, you should focus on the way you look.

Did your experiences seem more negative or positive? What do you feel like after taking a look at yourself? What kind of relationship do you share to your body? Take note of these thoughts when you reflect.

Favorite Features, Hated Features

What we feel physically attractive to ourselves or hate about ourselves can often hold an even deeper significance because how we view the way we look is connected to our sense of self-identity. Remember this when you write.

Five of your most-loved physical characteristics?

1.

2.

3.

4.

5.

Which do you consider to be your five least-favorite physical attributes?

1.

2.

3.

4.

5.

Self-Image Sketch

It was already clear the way you appear. Below Draw a sketch of what you think about yourself. This can help you start reflection about yourself. You shouldn't be thinking too much about the process. The process should be a natural one.

Do the exact drawing, however you must sketch an image of your shadow self, based upon the information you've learned in the past concerning shadow work. Don't overthink the method. Just let your ideas be natural.

Then looking at yourself from Afar

Consider how others could perceive the person you are. Based on the way you present yourself Write down what that other people may see about your character. This could differ from the way you view yourself or even how you view the shadow of yourself.

A Self History

Create a brief essay about the persona you were in your youth (How did you describe you back then? What prompted you to do so, etc.). Next, you should compare your childhood self-image with the way you portrayed yourself through the other activities (Are them the same? Different?).

The Importance of Identity

Your persona deserves your the time and consideration as it could have an array of positive influences on your personal life. If you're not sure your identity or try to conform to like the people around yourself, there's no way to promote confidence in yourself and the self-esteem is required to be successful. If someone isn't their own person, they are feeling distant from not only themselves as well as other people. Trust, confidence, healthy relationships, contentment as well as self-actualization are all benefits of knowing the person you are, and these factors can allow you to have a better life when you are able to cultivate them with shadow work.

Integrity is also a part of your identity as to behave ethically one must know the things you are devoted to. Integrity is the ability to live the values you hold dear. It is the way you apply your beliefs in all circumstances and even in the instances when it's difficult to follow through. Being honest is also a sign that you're willing to listen and adjust your beliefs based on the latest data. Values can not be separated from their surroundings and, therefore, even the same values are interpreted in different ways. The interpretation of the law is the sole responsibility that is the responsibility of Supreme Court. They don't alter the law but define what it means and what it means to apply to your situation. It is up to you to be aware of and understand your beliefs to live a morally sound life. In order to do that be able to do this, you must understand the dark parts of you as you understand the bright side.

Additionally, if you are aware of your identity and live your in accordance with your values, interactions will be stronger. It is well-known that doing shadow work can help to discover your own self-identity in new ways and once you're more comfortable within your self it also allows you to relate to others more easily. If you don't even know yourself, there's no chance to comprehend the other person. Learning to understand the shadow side of yourself helps you to become more comfortable with the unattractive parts of yourself. By accepting these parts of you it helps you to be more grounded and accept that you're not the perfect person and cannot believe that other people are flawless either.

If you are aware of who you are and what you want to be, you are able to act according to your true self. Your actions are no longer the way that society would expect. There are some societal rules which you must adhere to. But that doesn't mean that the society itself will define you. Your identity is unique that you have to embrace the aspects that make you one. There are aspects of you which the world won't be able to see and you have to explore and discover your shadow self to are aware of your inner motivations, and how your subconscious can oppose you, or help boost your joy and success. Your shadow self does not have to be a foe.

Self-actualization means that you are able to bring into your life the person you wish to become, and this is among the most transformational benefits of identifying your self. If you are aware of who you are and you are able to recognize what you would like and then make it happen. If you're not sure the things that appeal to you and what you want, it's hard to make it a reality. It's easier to achieve more by knowing yourself and you discover how to more effectively manage your time.

It is evident that discovering your identity is among of the most important things you can accomplish to yourself. It's just not so simple as it seems. It will take an enormous amount of work and effort to come back to yourself, especially if been spending a significant amount of the time pushing your inner self away, and attempting to avoid these thoughts. It's not enough to make your relationship with the subconscious aspect of yourself, and bring your thoughts back out to the light.

Virtue Checklist

Note down your top ten qualities that define your character.

1.

2.

3.

4.

5.

6.

7.

8.

9.

10.

What morals have been passed on to you through your parents? Are there morals that are contrary to your own family's morals? Take a look at the morals you've set up on your own and the ones you've been handed down and never doubted.

What Do You Want to Hide?

The shadow you create in your mind often attempts to conceal certain aspects of yourself which make you feel guilty, ashamed or any other negative emotions. It is possible to hide certain aspects of yourself due to the fact that you don't want them to exist. However, even though your self-identity is constantly changing there are certain aspects of you that won't disappear. the parts that are changing may be shifted however they're a the core of your identity so ignoring them won't cause them to disappear. The process of identifying your identity isn't just about taking care of the aspects of you that you are fond of but to fully discover what you're about it is necessary to confront your shadow self as well as all aspects of you that you do not like.

In some way, why individuals hide parts of their own. It's true that shame and things that we conceal have a lot in common. If we didn't feel shamed, we wouldn't be hiding portions of ourselves. What's more, there are people who feel ashamed of almost anything and the shame can come from a variety of different sources. Parents, our friends as well as society, can inform us that something's not right even though they might not intend to convey the message, however it is a common practice to internalize the message regardless.

If, for instance, one parent is always in the office trying to survive They may not be able to afford children the attention they want. Although the parent may be working hard and is in love with their child, they could be drawn into the lack of time and believe this has related to their worth. They'll seek to identify the flaws in their character in an attempt to get rid of the question of why they're not receiving the love they desire. The purpose of this scenario is not to assign blame, but to illustrate that shame and hurt aren't always a result of intent from others. The children develop the habit of making all of their own opinions about themselves. that can lead them to feel inadequate or experience shame because from who they are and the things they love about themselves.

Take a look at the distinction between guilt and shame. People often use both phrases interchangeably but there is a distinct distinction between the two. Brene Brown says that although guilt can be helpful but shame can be destructive. It is the feeling that you are guilty because you did something not right. When you, for example, steal the cookie you bought at a bake sale and feel guilty, it's a common sensation, reminding the person that they aren't doing something which is in line with your morals. In the same way, guilt is the recognition that you've done something wrong and shame is the sense that you're wrong but shame isn't always related to morality. People can be influenced by the messages of others that lead them to feel no matter what the cause they are inherently wrong with them.

Children are more prone to develop a sense of shame after they go through trauma and the shame that they experience can last for a long time after adulthood. In the case of the child is told either implicitly or explicitly or implicitly, that they're not loud enough, they might feel ashamed of their voice and even express them using the voice. In the same way, a child who has been abused might be embarrassed by what been done to them and they could believe that their abuse was not the fault of their parents. They'll think that they be guilty of something in order to merit this treatment. They are likely to search to find a flaw that could explain the neglect.

Adults are able to better understand that the abusive behavior is more related to someone else than they do but self-blame is an underlying problem for adulthood because it's more psychologically easy to believe that there's something going on with you rather than resolving the traumatizing emotions associated with violence and blame the other individual. Self-blame makes it easier to transfer the burden of your own suffering and provides you with more control over your pain however it may hurt you over the long term.

Though childhood shame is common however, it is possible to experience shame at any age, but typically, it begins early as new events can exacerbate and increase the severity of shame acute and affect other aspects in your daily life. Childhood shame could turn into shame for adults, and usually, the shame you feel can be a variant from the exact same situation.

The most painful part about being embarrassed is the fact that it won't improve your life as when you're embarrassed and ashamed, you don't deal with the root of the shame. The way you feel is that you are so ashamed of your self that it's uncomfortable to go through all those feelings and the causes that caused your guilt. However, to overcome your guilt, it is important to examine the root of your shame, and discover what is causing you to feel this the way you do. It is essential to expose the shame in order to be able to grow and make you show shame instead of honesty.

If we are feeling the shame of being a victim, we are tempted to conceal, but with shadow-work, we are able to express our feelings of guilt and shine spotlight on the issue. When we light the pit of shame, it becomes easier to realize that the pit isn't filled with the flaws of our own. It's full of hurt and childlike versions of us who are attempting to stay safe. It is a way to defend ourselves. It helps us to avoid the instances where we've been injured in the past by assuming responsibility of the hurt, regardless of whether it was the fault of us.

The benefit of working with shadows is the fact that you must face your guilt. Now is the time to take a look at yourself and start thinking "Why do I carry this shame?" These shadows are shameful parts. Once you are able to look at your shadow self, and begin looking at the useful prompts that are provided in this book, you will be able to be free of the burdens of shame. Parts of you that you are most prone to hiding are the ones that have to be exposed.

Meet the Stranger

Imagine the ways that you shield you from others. What strategies do you employ to conceal those areas?

Confession Time

Note down the ideas you've thought about in relation to shame. Think about what aspects of you make you feel the most nervous. Are you embarrassed about something? How do you are ashamed?

The Most Significant Shame The Greatest Shame or phase of your life which caused the greatest guilt.

Negative Trait List

Ten things you dislike about yourself.

1.

2.

3.

4.

5.

6.

7.

8.

9.

10.

Positive Traits

Ten traits you are proud of about yourself. These contrast with the negative aspects of you.

1.

2.

3.

4.

5.

6.

7.

8.

9.

10.

Who Am I?

You're ready to begin shaping your own identity. There is no way to just want to be different. It is essential to make the necessary steps to make that change happen. Already, you've made significant progress through the completed instructions, but you need to be able to dig further. Be aware that this journey takes the time. In the years that you've been repressing a part of yourself, you're probably not sure what you're really like overnight You're probably going to get more confused once you begin this journey, and the person you knew begins to clash with the new person who is who is emerging out of the darkness.

Be careful how you determine your identity. It is not necessary to hurry into the process. Journal entries aren't going to be the only thing that will provide immediate result. It will take time and dedication to discover the person you really are.

Do not forget the impact on other people. However, it is important to establish the boundaries that separate you and your influencers. Don't be confined to the opinions of others. As you begin to define your self You must ensure that you don't change and allow other people to determine your identity. You may seek out the support of others and advice however, ultimately, only individual can make the final decision on what you're really like. Take note of instances where individuals try to reveal about who you really are. They aren't necessarily trying to do so however, they've been exposed to certain characteristics and traits of you, as a result of the fear of self-doubt and shame there is a chance that you've hidden certain aspects of yourself beneath the cover of a disguise. So, determine what you really are and the person behind the disguise.

Keep in mind that you're constantly changing. You cannot "decide" who you want to be, and remain the same individual. It's inevitable that you'll change and that means you must be able to let your identity change with it also. It's not the same you who you were back in high school and don't need to become. There are still aspects of you which are the identical, but you've also acquired a wealth of knowledge and you're on the verge of becoming. Your attention is being paid to aspects you've missed, which makes a huge distinction.

Keep following the plan Even when it becomes difficult. Lessons are designed to complement one another It is essential to take these lessons with you and use them to enhance your performance in the future. And when you're feeling like that you're not yourself anymore take a look back at these lessons to refresh your self-esteem.

It is me...

Completing the sentences below.

When I wake up I am _____, and when I go to bed I am and I am _____ at home.

I am _____ after work, and I am _____ at home.

I am _____ with my family and _____ with my friends.

People tell me that I am _____, _____, and _____.

I am _____ most of the time.

I am _____, but I want to be _____.

I am ashamed of _____.

I am proud of _____.

I am feeling_____.

I am _____.

Write an Obituary

This may sound a bit morbid it's not, but composing an obituary of yourself is an excellent method of determining what you'd like to be remembered. Consider what you would like to be able to accomplish, and also the type of individual you'd like to become.

Personal Playlist

Make a playlist with 10 to 15 songs are what you consider to define who you are as an individual.

Chapter 9: Navigating Your Triggers

What Are Triggers?

In the case of emotional trauma or mental health problems Triggers may cause you to struggle with specific activities or environments However, as you become aware of your triggers you'll begin to fight them.Triggers are often scary and the term "trigger," unfortunately, is so popular that we often use around the idea without realizing just how harmful and damaging triggers could be to those who've been through their own. Triggers may prevent individuals from enjoying a full and joyful life as well as cause normal life to be scary and even painful. The root of triggers is within your shadow. The unconscious thoughts from your past triggers. That is the reason why working with shadows empowers individuals with triggers. There aren't any guarantees that everyone will be able to live without triggers However, through shadow work, you will master managing triggers.

Triggers are triggers that induce emotions. It is possible to become nervous, and panic attacks are often triggered by triggers however, there are a variety of different reactions that you could experience. A person who is someone who is an alcohol user, in the event of being confronted with an trigger may be tempted to drink, or a person with an eating disorder may wish to limit their intake of food or indulge in a binge eating habit. There are many feelings that you may experience such as despair, anger, or believe that your attempts are in vain. There is also the possibility of looking at yourself with a more negative perspective and have negative self-talk. This means you are saying hurtful or negative things about your self. The thoughts you have is when you're feeling triggered. It can be quite overwhelming and you might not be certain of how you should react. However, any trigger may have a long-lasting impact and can lead to an unhealthy mental state when they're not managed.

When you're feeling triggered it isn't like you're thinking your rational thinking You are often not aware of the situation, but various circumstances could trigger your. Certain triggers are fairly simple.

In the case of a victim, for example, someone that was victimized by shootings might be shaken at the sound of loud sounds which resemble gunshots. It's fairly obvious to make the link in this scenario However, certain triggers are more erratic. As an example, a child who was sexually victimized may get triggered by smells that are specific to them, but it could not immediately be evident that the smells are something to do with incidents of sexual assault. It is possible that the person does not be aware that, for example that a specific scent was one their victim was wearing. However, our senses possess remarkable memories, which is why certain triggers can be triggered by and even small stimuli.

Triggers vary, which is why it's very difficult to identify which triggers other people or trigger your own. If there were a magic method to solve triggers, it would seem easy. However, there's no method, and in order to comprehend triggers, it is necessary to recognize patterns and take an effort to note down how you react when you are being triggered.

Certain triggers are more easy to recognize than others, however, with keen observation and journaling, it is possible to determine the triggers that you are experiencing. Although you may know exactly the trigger that you are experiencing but you may not be able to pinpoint the reason, and need to recognize that memories aren't always clear as well. For all the sensations you recall you may have things you don't remember. That's okay. You just need to acknowledge the trigger, and be aware that it's an event. If you do eventually remember to mind, that's great however, if it does not then you do not need to recall every aspect of your trauma in order to heal this experience.

Trigger Log

Take note of moments when you're feeling stressed, and write the events down in a short note noting what occurred. When you record your observations and begin to identify patterns.

Confront Triggers

Although there are instances that can be prevented by avoiding triggers, you cannot keep avoiding certain situations forever and it's possible that you won't live life to the fullest until you can confront those triggers. If you are dealing with severe problems or have experienced trauma, this kind of therapy should be performed by someone to help you ground yourself and help you feel secure when you are doing this.

If you cannot or don't want professional assistance, having some the grounding methods read can help. As an example, you could engage in grounding activities like looking for objects in an area that have of a particular color or look through your body's senses and identify a handful of items that every sense could feel at this time. In many cases, confronting triggers means recalling the trauma of your past and dealing with negative experiences that have occurred to you. Therefore, at the very minimum, you should make certain that you've got someone to turn to (friend or partner.) who is ready to assist you.

It is already the first step in your trigger record. You are beginning to recognize your triggers. Once you have identified your triggers you are able to take a bit of confusion away. You are able to begin working with your inner self in order to discover the root of these triggers, and the reasons they keep causing your suffering.

When you feel triggered it is possible to do various options. Try an approach to grounding similar to the one mentioned below. It is also possible to contact a loved one. Also, making sure you're taking deep breaths helps to reduce anxiety. A few light physical exercises, particularly outdoors, may feel soothing as well. Cycling or an easy walk, slowly but consistently, is a great way to take your mind off of stressful emotions. Other hobbies that which you are passionate about can be great alternatives. Spend some time with yourself or pray (for people who practice religion) If you feel the need to. There is a lot you can do to relax yourself however, avoid any harmful behavior which will create more stress.

Recording your emotions is always beneficial. Examine what you felt as well as the underlying causes of these triggers. After you've identified the factors that trigger you, your process should concentrate on the way you reacted to the trigger and attempting to determine the message your inner self would like to convey. Making journal pages specifically for your inner self could assist to help, and later in the section, you will be able to explore your inner child. exercises will help you deal with any childhood traumas which could influence the triggers.

In reality When you face the triggers that you have, your initial action isn't simply to press into your trigger. It is important to analyze the circumstances and decide if you're prepared and secure to deal with your trigger.

A busy train station isn't an ideal location to deal with the trigger, and it could do more harm than beneficial. Additionally, if you've never looked at yourself inwardly towards your shadow self, you're not equipped to handle external triggers.

It is essential to have a broad awareness of what causes you to feel and what triggers you to effectively tackle triggers. After you've completed all the work you need to do, begin to expose yourself to those things that cause you to feel uneasy. Do this in a secure environment that is preferably in the company of people who will be there to support you should the need arises.

Be cautious when confronting the triggers. Begin by easing into the process then dip your feet in the water prior to deciding. Be prepared to confront the triggers that you are fighting for forever. However, be aware that you shouldn't throw yourself into something that panics your right away. Start by working with smaller triggers, and then progress to higher levels in the order you feel comfortable with.

Triggers to Confront

Record any triggers you'd like to overcome and write down your ideas on the best ways to deal with these triggers. What steps are you able to do to conquer your fears?

Chapter 10: Pain And The Inner Child
The Root of It All

Perhaps your childhood influenced you in many ways. The child within every one of us. It is a symbol of ourselves from the past. It is a symbol of the suffering we've been through as well as the present self we have created. It is not the case that everything goes back to your childhood however, a lot of the fundamental beliefs you hold about your world come from the earliest stages of your life, and it isn't easy to see the truth behind these views even when you've gained greater knowledge.

How was your environment at home as it was? The environment in which you live can affect the way a child develops to become an adult. If a home does not seem safe to a child, they is likely to carry the sense of fear with them and if the house is filthy, the child could find themselves feeling unclean. The space a child spends time within extends beyond their home. It can also include the places they are spending a significant amount of time. For instance, visiting relatives' homes at school, in the after-school, or during other events. Take a moment to think about some environmental factors that made you feel uncomfortable, inadequate or in any other way insecure. The shadow of you is a reflection of these feelings which means that even if you want to move forward, the anxieties of the past are always in the present.

Take a look at your caregiver. They may not always provide their children the things they require and sometimes this is intentional however, sometimes parents are unable or don't know what to do in order to provide their children with the items they require. The relationships with the caregivers of your children have been proven to be an excellent indicator of how your relationships with others as adults will look as. People who had parents that ensured that they felt secure and secure are more likely enjoy secure relationships with people due to the fact that they've been taught that secure relations are normal.

Children whose parents aren't attentive to their requirements, whether emotional or physical, are less secure within relationship. A few children possess a secure attachment, and others have an avoidant, anxious or anxiety-avoidant styles of attachment. These types of attachment can lead to many issues like an avoidant type can cause someone to flee whenever they believe that the other person isn't their ideal or be a threat to their safety, while an anxious style can lead a person to be too attached whenever they feel rejected. In the end, children learn to accept the connection they feel with their parents. However, the lessons they are taught isn't always grounded in logic and that's why parents may cause a lot of hurt to children.

The social connections you have outside the house can also affect how you develop your shadow. The importance of relationships is evident to everyone who are in good relationships, they will be able to manage better when faced with the rigors of trauma in the your home or at other places. In addition, poor relationships with others are often traumatic for children. Exclusion or bullying could make children feel excluded, that can cause anxiety. Families with healthy relationships are essential to the overall wellbeing of children, and the character of these relationships can be internalized.

Additionally, those who live marginalized or marginalized in the society generally are viewed as outcasts and have to struggle to be accepted. This can be extremely negative, and within certain societies, different people aren't always secure, and when people are different from the norm, they is a feeling of insecurity being a person. The feelings of insecurity can create trauma. This form of trauma is likely to create a lot of tension in children.

Childhood memories that are strong remain to you with a purpose. Some people don't remember their experiences well however for those that are able to, even being aware of what occurred to them could cause them to spiral, which is the reason why self-work shadows can be so difficult. When you are able to take a stand against the past and face them in your own way and then you begin to work with them, rather than being a slave to them. The memories you have will never be easy however, you shouldn't need to allow them to define the person you are.

Be prepared to reflect on your worst experiences of what has was happening to you. Most people try to avoid memories which they believe will cause them feel guilty. It's easy to push the memories aside, and convince yourself that you've got over it however, you're not. If you try to avoid something, it won't disappear. The issue remains in your mind's brain, and it will continue to affect your thoughts until you are able to address the issue.

The trauma you have experienced is a the basis of who you are. In the best or worst way the trauma you have experienced has shaped the way you view yourself. The perception of yourself as well as your behavior. Trauma wouldn't even be a problem even if it did not affect on you over the long run. Childhood trauma is often complicated and deeply ingrained however, that doesn't mean you should continue suffering.

It is essential to confront those issues from your childhood if are looking to improve your life. Do not force yourself to overlook or deny your grief. However, you shouldn't blame yourself for doing that previously. When you were younger, you didn't feel in a position to heal which is fine.

It was what you had to do to move through the past However, you're able to act differently today and focus on those dark areas of your life. These aren't as scary after you put a spotlight upon these dark areas. Be patient in the process and stop when you sense that your emotional turmoil is becoming excessive for you.

Guardian Thoughts

Consider your caretaker and the ways they attended or didn't attend to your needs during early children. What was it you wanted but they couldn't provide? Do you remember fondly the caregiver(s)? What do your caregivers expected from you? The answers to these questions could help to identify your emotional roots.

Childhood Fears

Think about the fears you faced when you were a kid.

First Memories

Consider your first bad memories (or your best guess of what might as your first) and then discuss the experiences you felt and feel in connection with those experiences.

The Power of Childhood Trauma

Other types of pain are among the toughest aspects of existence that can cause you feel more disconnected from your shadow self. The behavior you exhibit is in ways that reflect your past traumas however, you're not aware of the impact of this incident. A lot of people aren't aware the existence of trauma until they look into their own pasts and discover that they've been emotionally wounded during the past.

AS previously mentioned the fact that not every trauma is identical, and "small-t" trauma may not be as clear as it does not represent one event. Trauma in childhood can be more complicated because the child might not be aware of the proper boundaries, and also the difference between what was wrong and what is acceptable. As an example, a child that has been harmed by a predator could have difficulty reconciling seemingly pleasant actions and comprehend the reason the predatory behavior was a matter of course.

Before you can talk about trauma in depth, you need to understand what it is. Trauma, as a general term, is the psychological, emotional and physical way in which reacts to one incident or a series of incidents. Trauma may be emotional and physical, however this article will be focusing on the emotional consequences.

Trauma may cause anxiety, depression, Post-Traumatic Stress Disorder (PTSD) along with other mental health disorders. Whatever the way it manifests it can stop people from pursuing their dreams fully and can even push individuals away from their authentic self.

The effects of trauma last long after it initial occurrence. Trauma may have a variety of effects on individuals. As an example, a few individuals have mood fluctuations. Nightmares, relationship struggles and flashbacks are also possible. Others may experience physical signs like the feeling of shaking, heart racing or headache.

www.ingramcontent.com/pod-product-compliance
Lightning Source LLC
Chambersburg PA
CBHW070556010526
44118CB00012B/1333